THE READY RESOURCE FOR

Relief Society

—AND—

MELCHIZEDEK PRIESTHOOD

2019 CURRICULUM

Also by
TRINA BOICE

Base Hits and Home Run Relationships:
What Women Wish Guys Knew

My Future's So Bright, I Gotta Wear Shades

Bright Ideas for Young Women Leaders

Easy Enrichment Ideas:
Thinking Outside the Green Gelatin Box

Dad's Night: Fantastic Family Nights in 5 Minutes

Ready Resource for Relief Society:
2010, 2011, 2012, 2013, 2014, 2015, 2016, 2017

Ready Resource for Relief Society
and Melchizedek Priesthood:
2018, 2019

Sabbath Solutions: More Than 350 Ways
You Can Worship on the Lord's Day

Climbing Family Trees: Whispers in the Leaves

Great Ideas for Primary Activity Days

Parties with a Purpose:
Exciting Ideas for Ward Activities

Primarily for Cub Scouts

How to Stay UP in a DOWN Economy

You're What? 103 Creative Ways to
Announce Your Pregnancy

A Gift of Love—A Visual Pun Book of the Heart

Ancestry: How to Research Your Family
History and Climb Your Family Tree

THE READY RESOURCE FOR
Relief Society
—AND—
MELCHIZEDEK PRIESTHOOD
2019 CURRICULUM

TRINA BOICE

CFI
AN IMPRINT OF CEDAR FORT, INC.
SPRINGVILLE, UTAH

ISBN 13: 978-1-4621-2218-9

Published by CFI, an imprint of Cedar Fort, Inc.
2373 W. 700 S., Springville, UT 84663
Distributed by Cedar Fort, Inc., www.cedarfort.com

Library of Congress Control Number: 2018959490

Cover design by Shawnda T. Craig
Cover design © 2019 Cedar Fort, Inc.
Edited by Nicole Terry
Typeset by Kaitlin Barwick

Printed in the United States of America

10 9 8 7 6 5 4 3 2 1

Printed on acid-free paper

Contents

CONTENTS

Acknowledgments

I want to thank Cedar Fort for inviting me to share this annual book series adventure with them! I also want to send a big thank you to Katy Watkins, Kaitlin Barwick, Nicole Terry, and Shawnda Craig for all of their help with this edition.

A special thanks goes to my wonderfully supportive family for taking care of everything around me while I was busy pounding away at my computer keyboard. My husband and four sons inspire me to try harder and be better every day. I'm also forever grateful for my extended family's continued enthusiastic support, unconditional love, and kind encouragement.

Thank you to all the faithful members of the Church who valiantly magnify their callings and give of their time and talents to bless those around them. Heavenly Father knows that when we teach others, we learn more deeply ourselves. They say that God loves all people, but especially teachers because they remind Him of His Son!

Not only should we read the scriptures and have a meaningful gospel study plan, but also we're commanded to FEAST on the scriptures! It is my hope that this book serves as helpful utensils to enjoy your meal!

Introduction

The format for the 2019 lessons in Relief Society and priesthood quorums is designed to meet the unique needs of your ward or branch. This resource handbook will be a fantastic help for teachers and also for families and individuals who will be studying at home under the new "home-centered, Church-supported" program that was announced at the October 2018 general conference by President Russell M. Nelson.

The Ready Resource for Relief Society and Melchizedek Priesthood for 2019 has been created to be a helpful, inspiring resource to make lesson preparation easier and more tailored to meet the needs of your ward, branch, or family. The new *Come, Follow Me* manual can be obtained online for free and has been created by the Church to provide more flexibility for wards and branches all over the world to meet the unique needs of their members. Be sure to spend time reading it so that you can find the material that best serves your brothers and sisters. *The lesson suggestions in this resource book have been designed to focus on the Church's most-recent general conference talks in October and April 2018.*

Because the Church is growing rapidly and Saints are gathered across the globe, teachers will need to prayerfully consider the material that will be taught, focusing on the individuals in their class. The emphasis should be on ENGAGING classes and quorums in discussions rather than showcasing a teacher who does all of the talking. The more included people feel during a lesson, the more they will return to their homes edified and motivated to APPLY what they have learned and share it with their families.

The gospel means "good news" and should bring us great joy! Members of The Church of Jesus Christ of Latter-day Saints should be the happiest people around! May you feel the Savior's loving arms enfold you as you teach your dear brothers and sisters and feed His sheep!

Each chapter includes hymns appropriate for the lesson, quick summaries of the lesson material, quotes to supplement your class discussions, suggested artwork to display during your presentation, and object lessons to add pizzazz to your student participation. A feature in the book that encourages the members to immediately apply what they learn during your lesson is the weekly challenge. Two additional teaching tools that will strengthen spiritual growth and family relationships are the seminary doctrinal mastery passages (perfect for parents of teens) and correlating topics in the Church's missionary manual, *Preach My Gospel: A Guide to Missionary Service*, (perfect for parents of future and current missionaries). You're not teaching lessons—you're teaching your brothers and sisters!

In addition, each chapter contains a space to take personal notes and record inspiration as you prepare your thoughts. Former editions of *Ready Resource* included handouts. You can now find them at www.TrinasBooks.com. All of the quotes on this year's handouts come directly from the talks given at the October 2018 general conference.

The most important tool is the Holy Ghost, who will help you know how to tailor each lesson to meet the needs of your ward members and family.

Pray for the Holy Ghost to guide your study preparation before your lesson and for inspiration during your lesson. As you live the commandments and do your utmost to magnify your calling, you will receive personal revelation and direction on how you should share the lesson material to strengthen individuals and families.

The best lessons are not lectures but rather discussions where everyone participates. Try to involve the brothers and sisters in your class, encouraging them to share their experiences and testimonies of the principles you are teaching. They should leave your class feeling edified, enriched, and excited to live the gospel with joy!

Integrating various learning styles into your lessons improves attention and retention, assists in lesson planning, and inspires participants. Everyone learns differently, so be sure to include lots of variety in your teaching techniques. Try using some of the following ideas during your lessons:

STUDENT CENTERED

- Assignments
- Brainstorming
- Case studies
- Class Journals
- Crafts
- Debates
- Discussions
- Field Trips
- Games
- Instructional games
- Memorizing
- Note-taking
- Open-ended stories
- Oral reading
- Panels
- Questions
- Role-playing
- Songs
- Testimonies
- Worksheets

TEACHER CENTERED

- Catch phrases and tag lines
- Demonstrations
- Dramatization
- Feedback
- Guest speakers

- Jokes and puns
- Lectures
- Oral reading
- Personal emails
- Personal photos and videos

- Questions
- Storytelling
- Summarizing
- Surveys

MATERIALS CENTERED

- Artwork and photography
- Bulletin board
- Chalkboard
- Charts and maps
- Comics
- Creating original films
- Displays
- Dramatization

- DVDs
- eBooks
- Flannel board
- Flash cards
- Flip charts
- Graphs
- Handouts
- Mobile apps
- Overhead transparencies

- Posters
- PowerPoint presentations
- Puppet shows
- Quizzes and tests
- Social media
- Tape recording
- Treasure hunting
- Whiteboard

CHRIST CENTERED

- Building faith
- Church standards
- Devotionals
- Listen for the Spirit

- Prayer
- Scriptures
- Service projects
- Temple attendance

- Testimony
- Unconditional love

ARTWORK

Beautiful artwork can teach in a way that words alone cannot, especially for visual learners. Your church building's library may have some larger prints of older pictures that are numbered differently than what is in this reference book. Picture suggestions in this book will only include references to the Church's *Gospel Art Book*, which you can access for free online. Feel free to use any pictures that best illustrate your lesson.

You can also purchase the *Gospel Art Book* from Church Distribution at www.ldscatalog.com. It comes as a spiral-bound book containing 137 color pictures and a useful index that connects each image to the scriptures. It's an inexpensive and perfect investment for family home evening lessons! They are organized into the following six categories:

1. Old Testament
2. New Testament
3. Book of Mormon
4. Church History
5. Gospel in Action
6. Latter-day Prophets

You can access many pictures on the Church's website at www.lds.org/media-library/images. There you can also find cool memes (inspirational picture quotes), desktop wallpapers to let the members know about, and the ever-popular Mormonads.

The pictures online are organized into almost every category you can imagine. The site now allows you to create images and share your own photos and videos! Get in the habit of checking the Church's website often because there are always new features being added.

Some terrific Church resources that provide excellent artwork on gospel themes can also be found at the following websites:

- relarchive.byu.edu (BYU religious education image archive)
- josephsmith.net (Maps, artwork, photos, documents, and more about Joseph Smith and Church history)
- www.lds.org/temples/photo-gallery (Temple photos)

MUSIC

Music can effectively teach and can invite the Spirit better than almost any other teaching technique. Included with each lesson are suggestions for songs the class could learn from by singing or simply reading the lyrics. Inviting others in your ward to provide special musical numbers during your lessons binds hearts together and uplifts everyone. You can find the LDS hymnbook online at http://www.lds.org/churchmusic.

You can download songs, listen to them online, and do searches by topics, titles, and even scriptures! You can also use songs from seminary, Young Women, and Primary, as well as other music that has been published in Church magazines. Also on the Church's website are learning materials, such as how to conduct music, how to understand symbols and terms, and where to find great ideas to add variety to singing.

Check out these great resources:

- freewardchoirmusic.com (Free LDS musical arrangements)
- www.soundsmithmusic.com (Free LDS music)

QUOTES

Quotes from Church authorities can be used to inspire the mind and uplift the heart. It's nice to have some quotes written on the board at the front of the room for students to read before class starts to set the tone and to get them thinking about the topic. Some of the suggested handouts available on www. TrinasBooks.com use such quotes, but you can also design your own handouts with your favorite quotes. You can do a search at www.lds.org with a keyword about the topic you're searching for. More can be found online at

- www.quotegarden.com
- www.thinkexist.com
- www.inspirational-quotes.info
- www.brainyquote.com
- www.quotationspage.com
- www.wisdomquotes.com

ARTICLES

What a blessing it is to read messages from Church leaders each month in the various Church magazines. Teach your class how to find material to share with their families during family home evening lessons or to help them prepare sacrament talks in the future. Each lesson in this book includes only a few suggested articles, but there are so many more! One of the biggest blessings of preparing your lessons each month will be the focused time you get to spend researching specific gospel topics. You will learn so much more than you'll ever have time to share with your class on Sunday! Teaching at Church is a wonderful excuse to truly immerse yourself in gospel study. Enjoy it!

OBJECT LESSONS

Object lessons capture the students' interest and increase understanding by teaching the concept in a unique way. The Savior often used physical objects that were familiar to His listeners to illustrate simple principles. Each lesson offers ideas for object lessons that could be an effective introduction to the topic or a fun way to keep the class engaged during class time.

VIDEOS

The Church has some excellent videos that can be found and downloaded to your computer. You'll need a projector and either a white wall or screen in order to share them with your class.

A fantastic series of videos that is available online is called "The Life of Jesus Christ Bible Videos." You can find them at www.lds.org/bible-videos, where new ones are often added. There you can also download a free mobile app for viewing.

YouTube hosts several channels of videos officially released by the Church as well:

- www.youtube.com/user/MormonMessages
- www.youtube.com/user/LDSPublicAffairs

You'll find a lot of other great LDS videos on YouTube that were uploaded by members of the Church. Many chapels have internet access, but be sure to do a test run with your equipment before you decide to include videos in your lesson. Keep in mind that your lessons shouldn't be entertainment focused; they should be Spirit focused.

CHALLENGES

A meaningful addition to each lesson is the use of a personal challenge that you can share with the members at the end of each lesson. Perhaps it should be called an "invitation for application." They need to APPLY what they've learned after they leave your classroom. If they don't USE the lesson material to improve their lives and strengthen their testimonies, then they aren't growing spiritually from your efforts. You can offer the suggested challenge, one of your own, or invite the class to choose their own personal goal that will allow them to delve deeper and stretch farther. In the end, we won't be judged by all of the religious trivia we can recite to the Lord at the judgment seat but by the Christlike qualities we have acquired. The Lord cares much more about what we are becoming than what we are doing.

DOCTRINAL MASTERY PASSAGES

To strengthen their homes and families, parents of seminary students may want to learn some of the same one hundred scripture passages that their teens are learning. Parents will probably remember when these scripture passages were called "Seminary Scripture Mastery." Teachers can mention which verses correlate with each lesson's topic. What a terrific tool it is to commit scriptures to memory together. You can see all of the seminary manuals and resources at http://www.lds.org/manual/seminary.

PREACH MY GOSPEL

The Church is currently experiencing a wonderful wave of missionaries as the Lord hastens His work. The *Preach My Gospel* manual is not just for full-time missionaries but also for all of us to know how to prepare others to learn more about the gospel. The Church recently updated the manual in June 2018 to include recent changes to Church programs and terminology, such as references to the former home teaching and visiting teaching programs and changes in family history policy and products.

To help the members in your ward become more familiar with this missionary guide, consider including topical passages and talk about how to share your lesson material with non-member friends. You can see a free copy of the manual at https://www.lds.org/manual/preach-my-gospel-a-guide-to-missionary-service.

RESOURCES

Visit the Church website's sections that are dedicated to the Relief Society and elders quorum resources, which can be found under the "Serve and Teach" menu tab on the home page at www.lds.org. When you click on "Resources," you will discover all kinds of fantastic tools to help you in your sacred calling! Click on "Leadership Training Library" to see even more helpful tools. There is so much to see there.

The steps suggested for how to prepare a lesson include:

1. Use approved lesson materials. The Church has created a new *Come, Follow Me* manual for the 2019 lessons. Be sure to spend time reading it so that you can choose the material that best meets the needs of your class members.
2. Seek the guidance of the Spirit.
3. Study your lesson in advance.
4. Consider the needs of your class members.
5. Organize the lesson.
6. Seek the gift of teaching.

Jesus was the Master Teacher. He still is! He cared deeply about each person He taught. He used variety, honesty, symbolism, and storytelling, and He challenged His listeners to make specific changes in their lives. The more you study and teach the gospel, the greater your own understanding will be.

Use the scriptures each time you teach, and encourage your class to feast upon their teachings. As you come to love the scriptures, your class will feel that passion and be inspired to feast upon them as well. Your task as a teacher is to invite the members of your class to come unto Christ. In order to do that effectively, you must create an atmosphere where the Holy Ghost will be welcome and able to testify to the hearts of your students.

You give voice to the gospel principles taught each week, but it is the testifying power of the Holy Ghost that touches hearts and transforms lives. May you feel the Spirit guide and direct you as you do your best to magnify this calling!

• •

ARTICLES ABOUT TEACHING WITH THE SPIRIT

Matthew O. Richardson, "Teaching after the Manner of the Spirit," *Ensign*, Nov. 2011.

W. Grant Bangerter, "Teaching by the Spirit," *Ensign*, May 1980.

Thomas S. Monson, "'The Spirit Giveth Life,'" *Ensign*, May 1985.

Henry B. Eyring, "Rise To Your Call," *Liahona*, Nov. 2002.

William D. Oswald, "Gospel Teaching—Our Most Important Calling," *Liahona*, Nov. 2008.

Dallin H. Oaks, "Gospel Teaching," *Ensign*, Nov. 1999.

Bruce R. McConkie, "The Teacher's Divine Commission," *Ensign*, Apr. 1979.

David M. McConkie, "Gospel Learning and Teaching," *Liahona*, Nov. 2010.

"Teach by the Spirit": https://www.lds.org/manual/teaching-in-the-saviors-way /part-2-teach-by-the-spirit/teach-by-the-spirit

Daniel K. Judd, "Nourished by the Good Word of God," *Ensign*, Nov. 2007.

VIDEOS ABOUT TEACHING WITH THE SPIRIT

"Teaching by the Spirit": https://www.lds.org/media-library/video/2015-01 -0310-teaching-by-the-spirit

"Prepare and Teach by the Spirit": https://www.lds.org/media-library/video /2015-12-3000-prepare-and-teach-by-the-spirit

"If We Teach by the Spirit": https://www.lds.org/media-library/video/2010 -07-142-if-we-teach-by-the-spirit

"Fundamentals of Gospel Teaching and Learning": https://www.lds.org /media-library/video/annual-mutual-theme/2-fundamentals-of-gospel-teaching-and-learning

"Teach Me to Walk in the Light": https://www.lds.org/media-library/video /2014-01-1000-teach-me-to-walk-in-the-light

"Learning and Teaching in the Home and the Church": https://www.lds.org /media-library/video/2014-06-002-learning-and-teaching-in-the-home -and-the-church-the-church

Lesson 1

PERSONAL REVELATION

. . . .

MUSIC

"How Wondrous and Great," *Hymns*, no. 267
"Joseph Smith's First Prayer," *Hymns*, no. 26
"Oh, Holy Words of Truth and Love," *Hymns*, no. 271
"The Seventh Article of Faith," *Children's Songbook*, 126b
"Search, Ponder, and Pray," *Children's Songbook*, 109

. . . .

SUMMARY

President Russell M. Nelson boldly stated in the April 2018 general conference, "In coming days, it will not be possible to survive spiritually without the guiding, directing, comforting, and constant influence of the Holy Ghost" ("Revelation for the Church, Revelation for Our Lives," *Ensign*, Nov. 2018). That's a powerful statement to which we had better give heed. What do we need to do or change in our lives so that we can not only hear the voice of the Lord but also recognize it and act on it?

A kind and loving Father in Heaven blesses us with revelation through the Holy Ghost to direct us on the right path during life. Revelation to the Church comes through the Lord's appointed prophet. Personal revelation flows to us through inspired prayer, feelings, and thoughts and is predicated upon our worthiness.

We gain our testimonies and daily instruction from God through revelation. One of our greatest challenges in life is to learn how to recognize the promptings of the Holy Ghost. The more you pray, study the scriptures, and obey the commandments, the more familiar you will become with the Lord's voice and how He speaks to you.

QUOTES

~◦ "The word of the Lord in the scriptures is like a lamp to guide our feet, and revelation is like a mighty force that increases the lamp's illumination manyfold." (Dallin H. Oaks, "Feasting on the Word," *Ensign*, Mar. 2003.)

~◦ "The spirit of revelation is real—and can and does function in our individual lives and in The Church of Jesus Christ of Latter-day Saints." (David A. Bednar, "The Spirit of Revelation," *Ensign*, May 2011.)

~◦ "Personal revelation is the way we know for ourselves the most important truths of our existence." (Robert D. Hales, "Personal Revelation: The Teachings and Examples of the Prophets, *Ensign*, Nov. 2007.)

~◦ "Receiving personal revelation is not a passive process. As we seek such revelations, we must prepare for these sacred experiences. President Spencer W. Kimball told us that 'God reveals himself to [people] who are prepared for such manifestations.'" (L. Lionel Kendrick, "Personal Revelation," *Ensign*, Sept. 1999.)

~◦ "Revelation is spiritual in nature rather than physical. We can only understand the things of the Spirit by communication with our spirit. The Prophet Joseph Smith explained: 'All things whatsoever God in his infinite wisdom has seen fit and proper to reveal to us, while we are dwelling in mortality . . . are revealed to our spirits precisely as though we had no bodies at all; and those revelations which will save our spirits will save our bodies.'" (L. Lionel Kendrick, "Personal Revelation," *Ensign*, Sept. 1999.)

GOSPEL ART

Building the Ark, 7
Jacob Blessing His Sons, 12
Moses and the Burning Bush, 13
Isaiah Writes of Christ's Birth, 22
The Annunciation: The Angel Gabriel Appears to Mary, 28
Stephen Sees Jesus on the Right Hand of God, 63
Lehi Prophesying to the People of Jerusalem, 67
The Liahona, 68
Lehi's Dream, 69
Enos Praying, 72

VIDEOS

"Receiving Revelation": https://www.lds.org/media-library/video/2012-01-003
-receiving-revelation
"Are the Heavens Sealed?": http://lds.org/library/display/0,4945,6635-1-4786
-6,00.html
"The Spirit of Revelation": http://lds.org/pages/the-spirit-of-revelation-2011
-04?lang=eng&query=revelation
"Seek the Guidance of the Spirit": http://lds.org/service/serving-in-the
-church/relief-society/leader-resources/sunday-relief-society-meetings
/seek-guidance-of-the-spirit?lang=eng&query=revelation+(collection%3a"
media")
"Daily Bread: Pattern": https://www.lds.org/media-library/video/youth-curri
culum/may-prophets-and-revelation

OBJECT LESSONS

➥ On one side of the room, post a sign that says, "Invites the Spirit," and on the other side of the room, post a sign that says, "Drives the Spirit away." Pass out slips of paper that have different things written on them, such as reading the scriptures, watching TV, prayer, listening to classical music, watching a movie with lots of violence, etc. Invite the people holding the papers to stand on the side of the room that best describes whether the activity invites the Spirit or drives the Spirit away.

- Blindfold someone in the class and have them taste or simply smell different kinds of food. Choose some familiar items, like an orange or lemon, as well as some items that not everyone may know, like cilantro or star fruit. After the experiment, talk about how we can recognize revelation when we are already familiar with the Lord's voice and have experience with hearing it in our hearts or in our minds.

ARTICLES

Bruce R. McConkie, "How to Get Personal Revelation," BYU Devotional, Oct. 1966.

Dallin H. Oaks, "Eight Ways God Can Speak to You," *New Era*, Sept. 2004.

Dallin H. Oaks, "Revelation," BYU Devotional, Sept. 1981.

Bruce R. McConkie, "The Lord's People Receive Revelation," *Ensign*, June 1971.

Boyd K. Packer, "Personal Revelation: The Gift, the Test, and the Promise," *Ensign*, Nov. 1994.

CHALLENGE

Choose a topic you want to have a greater testimony of, or ask a question that you need an answer to. Spend time each day researching that subject in the scriptures as well as searching online for talks by prophets or General Authorities. Next, pray for guidance and a greater portion of the Spirit. Most importantly, listen in your heart and in your head for an answer.

DOCTRINAL MASTERY PASSAGES

Book of Mormon
2 Nephi 32:3
2 Nephi 32:8–9
Moroni 10:4–5

Old Testament
Exodus 33:11
Proverbs 3:5–6

Isaiah 29:13–14
Amos 3:7

New Testament
Matthew 16:15–19
Acts 7:55–56
2 Timothy 3:16–17

Doctrine and Covenants   D&C 137:7–10
D&C 8:2–3

● ●

PREACH MY GOSPEL

Pages 3, 18, 31, 32, 38, 44, 89, 90, 92–102

● ●

NOTES

_____

_____

_____

_____

_____

_____

_____

_____

_____

_____

_____

_____

_____

_____

_____

_____

_____

Lesson 2

THE COVENANT PATH

• •

MUSIC

"Father in Heaven, We Do Believe," *Hymns*, no. 180
"I Believe in Christ," *Hymns*, no. 134
"Nephi's Courage," *Children's Songbook*, 120
"Sweet Is the Peace the Gospel Brings," *Hymns*, no. 14
"We Give Thee But Thine Own," *Hymns*, no. 218

• •

SUMMARY

Being firm and steadfast in the faith of Christ was a common thread that ran through all of the talks given in the October 2018 general conference. Elder Dale G. Renlund stated in his talk, "God established a plan whereby we can become heirs in His kingdom, a covenant path that leads us to become like Him, have the kind of life He has, and live forever as families in His presence" ("Choose You This Day," *Ensign*, Nov. 2018).

In his talk, Elder D. Todd Christofferson encouraged us to stay on the covenant path when he said, "To persevere firm and steadfast in the faith of Christ requires that the gospel of Jesus Christ penetrate one's heart and soul" ("Firm and Steadfast in the Faith of Christ," *Ensign*, Nov. 2018). This is not a Sunday-only effort. Religion isn't just something we believe on the Sabbath day, but it is truly the blueprint for how we live our daily lives.

The gospel of Jesus Christ isn't about learning interesting scriptural facts or debating doctrine, but rather it is about applying those principles to our behavior and becoming Christlike in all that we say and do. Heavenly Father cares more about who we are than what we know.

Integrity is doing what we know to be true. Hypocrisy is when we go to church one day and act like nonbelievers the other six days of the week. We can't live worldly lives and then expect heavenly rewards. As members of the Church, we are expected to learn the gospel, live it, and share it. It should be our goal to progress from knowing to doing to becoming.

QUOTES

- "The blessings flowing from the observance of covenants are sufficiently great to recompense for all mere inconveniences." ("Messages of the First Presidency," vol. 6, 288.)
- "We are a covenant people. If there is a distinguishing feature about members of the Church, it is that we make covenants. We need to be known as a covenant-*keeping* people as well. Making promises is easy, but to follow through and do what we have promised is another matter." (F. Burton Howard, "Commitment," *Ensign*, May 1996.)
- "Making and keeping covenants means choosing to bind ourselves to our Father in Heaven and Jesus Christ. It is committing to follow the Savior. It is trusting Him and desiring to show our gratitude for the price He paid to se us free through the infinite gift of the Atonement." (Linda K. Burton, "The Power, Joy, and Love of Covenant Keeping," *Ensign*, Nov. 2013.)
- "The Christ-centered life produces in us, not a woeful countenance, but a disciplined enthusiasm to work righteousness." (Neal A. Maxwell, "The Christ-Centered Life," *Ensign*, Aug. 1981.)
- "At times we may rationalize that the Lord will understand our disobedience because our special circumstances make adherence to His laws difficult, embarrassing, or even painful. However, faithful obedience, regardless of the apparent size of the task, will bring the Lord's guidance, assistance, and peace." (Bruce A. Carlson, "When the Lord Commands," *Ensign*, May 2010.)

GOSPEL ART

Adam and Eve Kneeling at an Altar, 4
Adam and Eve Teaching Their Children, 5
City of Zion Is Taken Up, 6
The Ten Commandments, 14
Moses and the Brass Serpent, 16

VIDEOS

"My Covenant Path": https://www.lds.org/media-library/video/2014-01-180
-my-covenant-path
"Keeping Covenants Protects Us, Prepares Us, and Empowers Us": https://
www.lds.org/media-library/video/2014-03-0010-rosemary-m-wixom
"Walk in His Light": https://www.lds.org/media-library/video/2014-03-00
40-video-presentation-walk-in-his-light?category=youth-curriculum/07
-july
"We Believe: Theme Song": http://lds.org/media-library/video/strength-of
-youth-media

OBJECT LESSONS

↪ Divide the class into small groups. Give each group one specific covenant (e.g. baptism, confirmation, priesthood, sacrament, marriage, temple endowment) to dive deep into and later share with the rest of the class. Ask the groups to describe what is required of us and what the Lord promises us. Don't just talk about the behaviors, but dig deeper to talk about what qualities we must possess in the process.

↦ Fill some small brown lunch bags with various prizes, some good and some gag. Invite volunteers to choose which bag they would like. You could even have them recite a scripture or sing a song to "win" the prize. Compare the randomness of the quality of prizes with the security of making covenants with the Lord by explaining that we always know what the reward is for our obedience.

ARTICLES

Bonnie D. Parkin, "Celebrating Covenants," *Ensign*, May 1995.
Susan Bednar, "Covenant Blessings and Responsibilities," BYU–Idaho Devotional, Feb. 2002.
Paul V. Johnson, "Our Covenants Are Our Protection," BYU–Idaho Devotional, Nov. 2001.
D. Todd Christofferson, "The Power of Covenants," *Ensign*, May 2009.
M. Russell Ballard, "Keeping Covenants," *Ensign*, May 1993.

CHALLENGE

Make a list of all of the covenants you have made with the Lord, and rate how you are doing with your promises on a scale from one to ten. Next, write what changes you need to make in order to achieve a score of ten. Be honest with yourself. If you have received your temple endowment, ponder the questions that are asked in a temple recommend interview and evaluate your answers on the same scale.

DOCTRINAL MASTERY PASSAGES

Book of Mormon
1 Nephi 3:7
1 Nephi 19:23
2 Nephi 2:27
2 Nephi 32:3

2 Nephi 32:8–9
Jacob 2:18–19
Mosiah 4:30
Alma 32:21
Alma 34:32–34

Moroni 10:4–5

Old Testament
Exodus 20:3–17
Joshua 1:8
Psalms 24:3–4
Proverbs 3:5–6
Isaiah 29:13–14
Ezekiel 37:15–17
Daniel 2:44–45

New Testament
Matthew 16:15–19
John 7:17
John 14:15
John 17:3
Ephesians 4:11–14

Doctrine and Covenants
D&C 1:37–38
D&C 14:7
D&C 82:10
D&C 130:20–21

PREACH MY GOSPEL

Pages 8, 22, 25, 31, 32, 38, 39, 54, 61, 66, 72, 75, 76, 88, 121

NOTES

_____

_____

_____

_____

_____

_____

_____

_____

_____

_____

_____

_____

Lesson 3

GOSPEL STUDY
IN THE HOME

MUSIC

"Teach Me To Walk in the Light," *Hymns*, no. 304
"Thy Holy Word," *Hymns*, no. 279
"As I Search the Holy Scriptures," *Hymns*, no. 277
"Book of Mormon Stories," *Children's Songbook*, 118
"From Homes of Saints Glad Songs Arise," *Hymns*, no. 297
"The Books in the Book of Mormon," *Children's Songbook*, 119
"Welcome, Welcome, Sabbath Morning," *Hymns*, no. 280

SUMMARY

The October 2018 general conference introduced a "new balance between gospel instruction in the church and the home." President Russell M. Nelson explained, "It is time for a home-centered Church, supported by what takes place inside our branch, ward, and stake buildings" ("Opening Remarks," *Ensign*, Nov. 2018). "Church" and "religion" should take place in our homes and hearts rather than only in our meetinghouses.

It is vital to our children's salvation that we, as parents, not only introduce them to the scriptures but also show them how to search the scriptures, understand them, ascertain their truthfulness, and apply the teachings to their lives. The more we know, the better we will be able to make wise choices, help our families, and contribute to society.

Be sure to spend time with your class going over the new *Come, Follow Me* resource for individuals and families at https://www.lds.org/languages

/eng/content/manual/come-follow-me-for-individuals-and-families-new
-testament-2019/intro.

There are so many exciting things to learn! The Lord has commanded us to educate our minds, hearts, and hands (see D&C 88:78–80). As members of the Church, we should be an ever-learning people—not just a learned people. Having an earnest desire for truth can create a powerful experience when we search the sacred pages of scripture. The Lord has preserved in holy writ the information He knows will help us in mortality and lead us to Him. We can find more comfort and wisdom in the scriptures than in all other books ever written.

• •

QUOTES

- "Learning about sacred things should come first, providing a context and need for secular learning. If we want to return to our Heavenly Father's presence, our first priority should be to learn about his ways and his plan. The world would want to fool us into believing that there is insufficient time to engage in both spiritual and secular learning. I warn us not to be deceived by these philosophies of men. Our learning about sacred things will facilitate, even accelerate, our secular learning." (L. Tom Perry, "Learning to Serve," *Ensign*, Aug. 1996.)

- "Don't yield to Satan's lie that you don't have time to study the scriptures. Choose to take time to study them. Feasting on the word of God each day is more important than sleep, school, work, television shows, video games, or social media. You may need to reorganize your priorities to provide time for the study of the word of God. If so, do it!" (Elder Richard G. Scott, "Make the Exercise of Faith Your First Priority," *Ensign*, Nov. 2014, 93.)

- "Through reading the scriptures, we can gain the assurance of the Spirit that that which we read has come of God for the enlightenment, blessing, and joy of His children." (Gordon B. Hinckley, "Feasting upon the Scriptures," *Tambuli*, June 1986, 2–4; or *Ensign*, Dec. 1985, 42–45.)

- "The holy scriptures are like letters from home telling us how we can draw near to our Father in Heaven." (Ardeth G. Kapp, "The Holy Scriptures: Letters from Home," *Ensign*, Nov. 1985, 93–95.)

- "If you have not already developed the habit of daily scripture study, start now and keep studying in order to be prepared for your responsibilities in this life and in the eternities." (Julie B. Beck, "My Soul Delighteth in the Scriptures," *Liahona*, May 2004, 107–9; or *Ensign*, May 2004, 107–9.)

↦ "As a person studies the words of the Lord and obeys them, he or she draws closer to the Savior and obtains a greater desire to live a righteous life." (Merrill J. Bateman, "Coming unto Christ by Searching the Scriptures," *Ensign,* Nov. 1992, 27–28.)

GOSPEL ART

Adam and Eve Teaching Their Children, 5
Boy Jesus in the Temple, 34
Mary and Martha, 45
King Benjamin Addresses His People, 74
Two Thousand Young Warriors, 80
Jesus Blesses the Nephite Children, 84
Joseph Smith Seeks Wisdom in the Bible, 89
Young Boy Praying, 103
Family Prayer, 112
Young Couple Going to the Temple, 120

VIDEOS

"Seek Learning": https://www.lds.org/media-library/video/2012-03-1020-seek-learning
"Learning and Teaching in the Home and the Church": https://www.lds.org/media-library/video/2014-06-002-learning-and-teaching-in-the-home-and-the-church-the-church
"Learning with Our Hearts": https://www.lds.org/media-library/video/2012-10-1180-learning-with-our-hearts?category=standards-standards/education-standards
"Standards: Education—The Glory of God Is Intelligence": https://www.lds.org/media-library/video/2012-10-012-standards-education-the-glory-of-god-is-intelligence?category=standards-standards/education-standards
"Study the Scriptures": https://www.lds.org/manual/preach-my-gospel/asl/chapter3/lesson4?lang=eng#study-the-scriptures
"Learn about Scriptures": https://www.lds.org/pages/learn-about/scriptures
"King James Bible Anniversary": https://www.lds.org/media-library/video/2011-04-28-king-james-bible-anniversary
"Scriptures—More Precious than Gold and Sweeter Than Honey": https://www.lds.org/media-library/video/2005-09-04-scriptures-more-precious-than-gold-and-sweeter-than-honey

• •

OBJECT LESSONS

•→ Divide the class into groups and pass out three-by-five-inch index cards that have the words to a scripture written on one side and a different kind of snack written on the back. When the groups memorize the scripture, they get the snack. Show them how this could be a fun activity to do at home with their kids. Another option would be to invite each group to show a creative way to teach their assigned scripture passage to their family.

•→ Bring a plate of cookies, and ask for volunteers to demonstrate different styles of eating: abstain, sample, taste, snack, gorge, nibble, eat, and feast. Now compare those styles to how we study the scriptures, reminding the class that we should "feast upon the words of Christ" (2 Nephi 32:3).

•→ Ask a class member to play a hymn on the harmonica. (Pick someone who doesn't know how to play it.) When the class member explains that he or she can't do it, ask the class how he or she could learn. "Study a manual" or "Learn from someone who can" are correct answers. The same applies to learning to be like Heavenly Father; we can learn about Him in the scriptures, and we can follow the Savior, who is like Him. Daily practice makes perfect!

• •

ARTICLES

David A. Bednar, "Learning to Love Learning," *Ensign*, Feb. 2010.

Gordon B. Hinckley, "Words of the Prophet: Seek Learning," *New Era*, Sept. 2007.

Dallin H. Oaks, "Learning and Latter-day Saints," *Liahona*, Apr. 2009.

Mary N. Cook, "Seek Learning: You Have a Work to Do," *Ensign*, May 2012.

Thomas S. Monson, "To Learn, to Do, to Be," *Ensign*, Nov. 2008.

Dallin H. Oaks, "Feasting on the Word," *Ensign*, Mar. 2003, 35–36.

Henry B. Eyring, "A Discussion on Scripture Study," *Ensign*, July 2005.

Dallin H. Oaks, "Scripture Reading and Revelation," *Ensign*, Jan. 1995.

Julie B. Beck, "My Soul Delighteth in the Scriptures," *Ensign*, May 2004.

Richard J. Maynes, "Establishing a Christ-Centered Home," *Ensign*, May 2011.

Lawrence E. Corbridge, "Valiant in the Testimony of Jesus Christ," *Ensign*, Sept. 2011.

• •

CHALLENGE

Listen to an episode of the Gospel Principles podcast at http://feeds.lds.org/tptc_JS_mp4_ase while you mark seminary doctrinal mastery passages in your scriptures. Begin memorizing them with your family. Have an old-fashioned scripture chase! That's a game seminary students have played for many years. The teacher gives clues, and the students race to see who can find the correct scripture the fastest.

• •

DOCTRINAL MASTERY PASSAGES

Book of Mormon
1 Nephi 19:23
2 Nephi 9:28–29
2 Nephi 32:3
2 Nephi 32:8–9
Jacob 2:18–19
Mosiah 2:17
Alma 34:32–34
Alma 37:6–7
Alma 37:35
Helaman 5:12
3 Nephi 27:27
Moroni 7:16–17
Moroni 10:4–5

Old Testament
Exodus 20:3–17
Deuteronomy 7:3–4
Joshua 24:15
Job 19:25–26
Proverbs 3:5–6
Isaiah 29:13–14

Isaiah 53:3–5
Isaiah 55:8–9
Daniel 2:44–45

New Testament
Matthew 6:24
Luke 24:36–39
John 7:17
John 14:15
John 17:3
Ephesians 4:11–14
2 Timothy 3:16–17
Revelation 20:12–13

Doctrine and Covenants
D&C 14:7
D&C 76:22–24
D&C 89:18–21
D&C 137:7–10

Joseph Smith—History
JS—H 1:15–20

• •

PREACH MY GOSPEL

Pages 1, 5, 33, 37, 46, 48, 51–54, 60–61, 90, 105, 108, 115–116, 123–126, 198–199

• •

NOTES

_____

_____

_____

_____

_____

_____

_____

_____

_____

_____

_____

_____

_____

_____

_____

_____

_____

_____

_____

_____

_____

Lesson 4

TAKING UPON US THE NAME OF JESUS CHRIST

. . . .

MUSIC

"Come, All Ye Sons of God," *Hymns*, no. 322

"For All the Saints," *Hymns*, no. 82

"Israel, Israel, God Is Calling," *Hymns*, no. 7

"I Know That My Redeemer Lives," *Hymns*, no. 136

"Jesus, Lover of My Soul," *Hymns*, no. 102

"I'm Trying to Be Like Jesus," *Children's Songbook*, 78

"The Lord Is My Light," *Hymns*, no. 89

"Come unto Jesus," *Hymns*, no. 117

. . . .

SUMMARY

President Russell M. Nelson reminded us during the last several general conferences of the importance of using the correct name of the Church. He stated, "Jesus Christ directed us to call the Church by His name because it is His Church, filled with His power" ("The Correct Name of the Church," *Ensign*, Nov. 2018).

The name of the Church was given by Jesus Christ himself as a commandment (see D&C 115:4). When we use nicknames for the Church, we unwittingly remove the sacred name of Jesus Christ. The Church of Jesus Christ of Latter-day Saints offers the fulness of the gospel to the world today, and it is our responsibility to share it with the world and gladly proclaim that Jesus Christ is the center of it all.

QUOTES

★ "Taking the Savior's name upon us includes declaring and witnessing to others—through our actions and our words—that Jesus is the Christ. Have we been so afraid to *offend* someone who called us 'Mormons' that we have failed to *defend* the Savior Himself, to stand up for Him even in the name by which His Church is called?" (Russell M. Nelson, "The Correct Name of the Church," *Ensign*, Nov. 2018.)

★ "Let us develop the habit . . . of making it clear that The Church of Jesus Christ of Latter-day Saints is the name by which the Lord Himself has directed that we be known." (M. Russell Ballard, "The Importance of a Name," *Ensign*, Nov. 2011.)

★ "If members learn to use the correct name of the Church, . . . it will underscore that we are Christians, members of the Savior's Church." (M. Russell Ballard, "Following Up," *Ensign*, May 2014.)

GOSPEL ART

Daniel Interprets Nebuchadnezzar's Dream, 115
Missionaries Teach the Gospel of Jesus Christ, 612
My Gospel Standards, 618

VIDEOS

"Taking upon Ourselves the Name of Jesus Christ": https://www.lds.org/media-library/video/2018-10-5030-robert-c-gay-1080p-eng
"What Does it Mean to Take upon Myself the Name of Jesus Christ?": https://www.lds.org/media-library/video/what-does-it-mean-to-take-upon-myself-the-name-of-jesus-christ-young-women
"Jesus Christ Names His Church": https://www.lds.org/media-library/video/2010-06-44-chapter-43-jesus-christ-names-his-church-april-1838

OBJECT LESSONS

★ Divide the class into groups, and play a trivia game, challenging them to name certain things (e.g. Academy Award winners, sports teams, university mascots, state capitals). After the game, talk about the importance of names. You could invite class members to talk about how difficult it was to choose names for their babies.

┅● Invite a newlywed couple to share a little bit about their wedding. Ask the bride why she changed her last name to her new husband's name, if she did. Ask her husband how that made him feel.

┅● Pass out gum to the class, and tell them to chew it for about five minutes to get all of the flavor out of it. Now ask the class to put it back into the wrapper and mold it into the original form. Explain that many men have tried to recreate Christ's true church. Only with the Savior's help was Joseph Smith able to restore the Lord's church. We learn in both the Doctrine and Covenants and the Book of Mormon that the Lord gave a specific name for the Church. Challenge the class to find those verses in both books of scripture.

ARTICLES

Russell M. Nelson, "The Correct Name of the Church," *Ensign*, Nov. 2018.

Robert C. Gay, "Taking upon Ourselves the Name of Jesus Christ," *Ensign*, Oct. 2018.

Russell M. Nelson, "Thus Shall My Church Be Called," *Ensign*, May 1990.

Dallin H. Oaks, "Taking upon Us the Name of Jesus Christ," *Ensign*, May 1985.

M. Russell Ballard, "The Importance of a Name," *Ensign*, Nov. 2011.

David A. Bednar, "Chosen to Bear Testimony of My Name," *Ensign*, Nov. 2015.

Marion G. Romney, "Why The Church of Jesus Christ of Latter-day Saints," *Ensign*, Jan. 1973.

CHALLENGE

Post something on any of your social media accounts about being a member of the Church. Use the correct name of the Church, and thank the readers for not using nicknames anymore.

DOCTRINAL MASTERY PASSAGES

New Testament
Ephesians 4:11–14

• •

PREACH MY GOSPEL

Pages 5, 46, 60

• •

NOTES

_____

_____

_____

_____

_____

_____

_____

_____

_____

_____

_____

_____

_____

_____

_____

_____

_____

_____

_____

_____

_____

Lesson 5

THE REDEMPTIVE POWER OF THE ATONEMENT OF JESUS CHRIST

• •

MUSIC

"Christ the Lord Is Risen Today," *Hymns*, no. 200
"God Loved Us, So He Sent His Son," *Hymns*, no. 187
"Behold the Great Redeemer Die," *Hymns*, no. 191
"In Humility, Our Savior," *Hymns*, no. 172
"Our Savior's Love," *Hymns*, no. 113
"I Know That My Redeemer Lives," *Hymns*, no. 136
"Jesus, Lover of My Soul," *Hymns*, no. 102
"I'm Trying to Be like Jesus," *Children's Songbook*, 78
"The Lord Is My Light," *Hymns*, no. 89
"Jesus, the Very Thought of Thee," *Hymns*, no. 141
"Come unto Jesus," *Hymns*, no. 117

• •

SUMMARY

The power of the Atonement was the focus of the October 2018 general conference. Elder Matthew L. Carpenter taught us about the healing power of the Atonement when he shared, "Because of the Atonement of Jesus Christ, if we choose to repent and turn our hearts fully to the Savior, He will heal us spiritually" ("Wilt Thou Be Made Whole?" *Ensign*, Nov. 2018).

Jesus Christ is the Only Begotten Son of God and the Savior of the world. He was chosen and foreordained to come to earth to atone for our sins and teach us how to return to our Heavenly Father. Our faith and hope are built upon the Savior's atoning sacrifice.

The most important event in the history of mankind was when the Savior was crucified for the world. Jesus Christ's Atonement took place in the Garden of Gethsemane and on the cross at Calvary. His redeeming sacrifice was necessary to ransom all people from the physical and spiritual effects of sin. Because of His merciful gift, we all have the opportunity to repent, be forgiven of our sins, and be resurrected. To thank Him for paying our spiritual and physical debts, we must show faith in Him, repent, be baptized, and follow Him.

QUOTES

- "I weep for joy when I contemplate the significance of it all. To be redeemed is to be atoned—received in the close embrace of God with an expression not only of His forgiveness, but of our oneness of heart and mind." (Russell M. Nelson, "The Atonement," *Ensign*, Nov. 1996.)
- "The Redeemer loves you and will help you do the essential things that bring happiness now and forever." (Richard G. Scott, "Jesus Christ, Our Redeemer," *Ensign*, May 1997, 53–54, 59.)
- "Ever and always [the Atonement] offers amnesty from transgression and from death if we will but repent. . . . Repentance is the key with which we can unlock the prison from inside . . . and agency is ours to use it." (Boyd K. Packer, "Atonement, Agency, Accountability," *Ensign*, May 1988, 69–72.)
- "[The Lord's] atonement is the most transcendent event that ever has or ever will occur from Creation's dawn through all the ages of a never-ending eternity." (Bruce R. McConkie, "The Purifying Power of Gethsemane," *Ensign*, May 1985, 9–11.)
- "The Savior's birth, ministry, atoning sacrifice, Resurrection, and promised coming all bear witness to His divinity." (Ezra Taft Benson, "Five Marks of the Divinity of Jesus Christ," *Ensign*, Dec. 2001, 8–15.)

GOSPEL ART

Isaiah Writes of Christ's Birth, 22
The Nativity, 30
Boy Jesus in the Temple, 34

VIDEOS

"Jesus Christ Suffered for Us": https://www.lds.org/media-library/video/2010-05-1150-jesus-christ-suffered-for-us

"He Is Not Here: for He Is Risen": https://www.lds.org/media-library/video/2013-10-1210-he-is-not-here-for-he-is-risen

"The Mediator": http://lds.org/library/display/0,4945,6635-1-4786-2,00.html

"To This End Was I Born": http://lds.org/media-library/video/new-testament-presentations

"Lifting Burdens: The Atonement": http://www.youtube.com/watch?v=coef8G5ax6E

OBJECT LESSONS

- Invite a class member to hold a Ping-Pong ball. Tell the person to let go of the ball and see what happens. Of course, it falls to the ground. Gravity is like sin that pulls us down. Now ask the person if he or she can keep the Ping-Pong ball to float in midair without touching it. Of course, it can't be done . . . or can it? Set a hair dryer on the cool setting and turn it on high while pointing it toward the ceiling. Carefully put the Ping-Pong ball into the air stream. If done correctly, the ball should float. The power of the hair dryer is like the Atonement of Jesus Christ; it allows us to float heavenward and defy the effects of sin.
- Pass out Tootsie Pops, and invite the class to share ways that the candy can teach us about the Atonement. Their answers will probably be pretty

creative and even entertaining. There are no wrong answers. If they haven't already mentioned some of these points, share them with the class after they have given their answers. The center of the candy is soft, like a person's heart. How does a heart become hard? (Possible answers: sin, trials, pain, pride, etc.) Some people cover their hard-heartedness with denial or pride (the paper wrapper over the candy), often in an attempt to hide what's in their hearts and to look good to others. When a person removes the wrapper of denial and pride, the Spirit can begin to work on the heart. Sometimes we have to take a few "licks" (trials) before our heart can be softened. The sweet Atonement gets to the center of our hearts and can change us into something moldable and good.

- Ask someone in the class to put on a sock. Hand the volunteer a muddy sock. The volunteer will probably not want to touch the dirty sock, so ask the volunteer what could be done to make him or her willing to put it on. After he or she has given an answer, tell the volunteer you'll take the muddy sock and give her a clean, new one. The Savior took upon Himself all of our dirty sins and gave us each a clean sock to wear when we return to our Father in Heaven so that we will be clean from the sins of the world.

ARTICLES

M. Russell Ballard, "The Atonement and the Value of One Soul," *Ensign*, May 2004.

Cecil O. Samuelson Jr., "What Does the Atonement Mean to You?" *Ensign*, Apr. 2009.

Marion G. Romney, "Christ's Atonement: The Gift Supreme," *Ensign*, Dec. 1973.

James E. Faust, "The Atonement: Our Greatest Hope," *Ensign*, Nov. 2001.

Dallin H. Oaks, "Strengthened by the Atonement of Jesus Christ," *Ensign*, Nov. 2015.

Kent F. Richards, "The Atonement Covers All Pain," *Ensign*, May 2011.

CHALLENGE

Write your testimony of the Savior and how you feel about the Atonement. Share it with your family, someone serving a mission, or a non-member. Like Nephi's small plates, begin a spiritual journal in which you write about faith-building experiences you are having in your life. This will become a source of inspiration for your posterity.

• •

DOCTRINAL MASTERY PASSAGES

Book of Mormon
Helaman 5:12
3 Nephi 27:27

Old Testament
Genesis 1:26–27
Job 19:25–26
Isaiah 53:3–5

New Testament
Matthew 16:15–19

Luke 24:36–39
John 3:5
John 17:3
Acts 7:55–56
1 Corinthians 15:20–22

Doctrine and Covenants
D&C 19:16–19
D&C 76:22–24
D&C 130:22–23

• •

PREACH MY GOSPEL

Pages 34, 37, 47–48, 51–52, 60–61, 90, 105, 116, 123–126

• •

NOTES

_____

_____

_____

_____

_____

_____

_____

_____

_____

Lesson 6

DEEPENING OUR CONVERSION

MUSIC

"I Know That My Redeemer Lives," *Hymns*, no. 136
"Jesus, Lover of My Soul," *Hymns*, no. 102
"I'm Trying to Be like Jesus," *Children's Songbook*, 78
"The Lord Is My Light," *Hymns*, no. 89
"Jesus, the Very Thought of Thee," *Hymns*, no. 141
"Come unto Jesus," *Hymns*, no. 117

SUMMARY

President Russell M. Nelson clearly stated in the October 2018 general conference, "The long-standing objective of the Church is to assist all members to increase their faith in our Lord Jesus Christ and in His Atonement, to assist them in making and keeping their covenants with God, and to strengthen and seal their families" ("Opening Remarks," *Ensign*, Nov. 2018).

Jesus Christ was not just a good man, an effective teacher, or inspiring leader; He is the Redeemer of the world! As members of the Church, we believe not only that the Savior lived on this earth and died for our sins but also that He still lives! Our lives should reflect those beliefs. Our actions should testify to all that we know He is coming again soon.

By following Jesus Christ we can receive peace in this life and eternal joy in the life to come. We can build a testimony of Him through scripture study, prayer, and following His example. As we learn more about the Savior, our desire to be more like Him will increase.

QUOTES

-• "The stories of Jesus can be like a rushing wind across the embers of faith in the hearts of our children. Jesus said, 'I am the way, the truth, and the life.' The stories of Jesus shared over and over bring faith in the Lord Jesus Christ and strength to the foundation of testimony. Can you think of a more valuable gift for our children?" (Neil L. Andersen, "Tell Me the Stories of Jesus," *Ensign*, May 2010.)

-• "Each of us has the responsibility to know the Lord, love Him, follow Him, serve Him, teach and testify of Him." (Russell M. Nelson, "Jesus the Christ: Our Master and More," *Liahona*, Apr. 2000, 4–19; or *Ensign*, Apr. 2000, 4–17.)

-• "The soul that comes unto Christ dwells within a personal fortress, a veritable palace of perfect peace." (Jeffrey R. Holland, "Come unto Me," *Ensign*, Apr. 1998.)

-• "To follow Christ is to become more like Him. It is to learn from His character. As spirit children of our Heavenly Father, we do have the potential to incorporate Christlike attributes into our life and character." (Dieter F. Uchtdorf, "Developing Christlike Attributes," *Ensign*, Oct. 2008.)

GOSPEL ART

Isaiah Writes of Christ's Birth, 22
The Nativity, 30
Boy Jesus in the Temple, 34
John the Baptist Baptizing Jesus, 35
Calling of the Fishermen, 37
Christ Ordaining the Apostles, 38
The Sermon on the Mount, 39
Jesus Blessing Jairus's Daughter, 41
Christ Walking on the Water, 43
Mary and Martha, 45
Christ and the Rich Young Ruler, 48
Triumphal Entry, 50
Jesus Washing the Apostles' Feet, 55
Jesus Praying in Gethsemane, 56
The Crucifixion, 57
Burial of Jesus, 58

• •

VIDEOS

There are many videos to choose from in the Church's new Bible videos about the life of Jesus Christ found at https://www.lds.org/bible-videos
"Jesus Declares He Is the Messiah": https://www.lds.org/media-library/video/2011-10-029-jesus-declares-he-is-the-messiah
"Are We Christians?": https://www.lds.org/pages/mormon-messages
See some of the great testimonies of Christ on www.mormonchannel.org/video under "I'm a Mormon," "Bible Videos," and "New Testament Stories."

• •

OBJECT LESSONS

↝ Show pictures of various objects, and ask the class how the objects relate to Jesus Christ:
   » Porch light: serves as a beacon to help us find our way home
   » Campfire: provides warmth and comfort
   » Lighthouse: offers light in the darkness, offers perspective in the storm
   » Night light: banishes darkness and eliminates fear
   » Car headlights: let us know where we are heading
   » Lights in a movie theater: guide that can be followed
   » Light bulb: inspires us, and brings us new light and understanding
↝ Ask for a volunteer to stand in a square that is marked on the floor with masking tape. Show him or her a candy bar on the table out of his or her reach, and tell the volunteer that he or she can have it only if he or she can reach it without leaving the square. After the volunteer tries and fails, ask for another volunteer to help him or her. That's what the Savior did for us; He bridges the gap between mortality and eternal life. He gave us the

gift of repentance through His Atonement so we can taste the sweet love of Heavenly Father!

- ⇢ Set out pictures of the Savior around the room. Invite the class to select one and talk about it. The class's comments will turn into a very sweet testimony meeting about the Savior.
- ⇢ Show the class two pictures that seem very much alike but have a few differences. Have the class point out the differences. In order to align our life with the Lord's, we need to follow His example, which we can find in the scriptures, and change our lives to match His model for us.

ARTICLES

Dieter F. Uchtdorf, "Behold the Man!" *Ensign*, May 2018.

James M. Paramore, "The Many Witnesses of Jesus Christ and His Work," *Ensign*, Nov. 1990.

Gary J. Coleman, "Jesus Christ Is at the Center of the Restoration of the Gospel," *Ensign*, Nov. 1992.

Ezra Taft Benson, "Five Marks of the Divinity of Jesus Christ," *Ensign*, Dec. 2001.

Ezra Taft Benson, "Jesus Christ: Our Savior and Redeemer," *Ensign*, June 1990.

Russell M. Nelson, "Jesus the Christ: Our Master and More," *Ensign*, Apr. 2000.

Orson F. Whitney, "The Divinity of Jesus Christ," *Ensign*, Dec. 2003.

CHALLENGE

Write your testimony of Jesus Christ in your journal, and share it with your family. Write it in a Book of Mormon, and share it with a non-member.

DOCTRINAL MASTERY PASSAGES

Book of Mormon
Helaman 5:12
3 Nephi 27:27

Old Testament
Genesis 1:26–27
Job 19:25–26
Isaiah 53:3–5

New Testament
Matthew 16:15–19
Luke 24:36–39
John 3:5
John 17:3
Acts 7:55–56
1 Corinthians 15:20–22

Doctrine and Covenants   D&C 76:22–24
D&C 19:16–19   D&C 130:22–23

• •

PREACH MY GOSPEL

Pages 34, 37, 47–48, 51–52, 60–61, 90, 105, 116, 123–126

• •

NOTES

_____

_____

_____

_____

_____

_____

_____

_____

_____

_____

_____

_____

_____

_____

_____

_____

Lesson 7

CREATING SANCTUARIES OF FAITH

. . . .

MUSIC

"Go Forth with Faith," *Hymns*, no. 263
"Faith of Our Fathers," *Hymns*, no. 84
"Testimony," *Hymns*, no. 137
"When Faith Endures," *Hymns*, no. 128
"True to the Faith," *Hymns*, no. 254

. . . .

SUMMARY

The October 2018 general conference introduced a new "balance between home and church." President Russell M. Nelson inspired us when he said, "The new home-centered, Church-supported integrated curriculum has the potential to unleash the power of families, as each family follows through conscientiously and carefully to transform their home into a sanctuary of faith" ("Becoming Exemplary Latter-day Saints," *Ensign*, Nov. 2018).

The first principle of the gospel is faith in the Lord Jesus Christ. Faith is believing in Him with our spiritual eyes when we haven't seen Him with our physical eyes. It is a principle of action that compels us to pray, be obedient, and trust in His promises. We increase our faith by testing and studying His words. Faith has power to move mountains, perform miracles, and prove us worthy to see God.

Our faith can provide the light we need to live in a dark world. When doubts begin to enter our minds and hearts, we need to hold on to the things we know to be true, and the Lord will help us to build on that foundation.

QUOTES

➤ "Three principles that will help you strengthen your home and family are nurturing, sacrifice, and prayer." (Carol B. Thomas, "Strengthen Home and Family," *Ensign*, May 2002.)

➤ "The health of any society, the happiness of its people, their prosperity, and their peace all find common roots in the teaching of children in the home." (L. Tom Perry, "Mothers Teaching Children in the Home," *Ensign*, May 2010.)

➤ "Spiritual light rarely comes to those who merely sit in darkness waiting for someone to flip a switch. It takes an act of faith to open our eyes to the Light of Christ. Spiritual light cannot be discerned by carnal eyes." (Dieter F. Uchtdorf, "The Hope of God's Light," *Ensign*, May 2013.)

➤ "Faith is not only a feeling; it is a decision." (Neil L. Andersen, in Conference Report, *Ensign*, Nov. 2008, 14.)

➤ "Only faith in the Lord Jesus Christ and His Atonement can bring us peace, hope, and understanding." (Robert D. Hales, "Finding Faith in the Lord Jesus Christ," *Liahona*, Nov. 2004, 70–73; or *Ensign*, Nov. 2004, 70–73.)

➤ "We promote the process of strengthening our faith when we do what is right—increased faith always follows." (L. Whitney Clayton, "'Help Thou Mine Unbelief,'" *Liahona*, Jan. 2002, 31–33; or *Ensign*, Nov. 2001, 28–29.)

➤ "Faith in Jesus Christ takes us beyond mere acceptance of the Savior's identity and existence. It includes having complete confidence in His infinite and eternal redemptive power." (James O. Mason, "Faith in Jesus Christ," *Ensign*, Apr. 2001, 22–27.)

➤ "Faith in the Lord Jesus Christ is a conviction and trust that God knows us and loves us and will hear our prayers and answer them with what is best for us." (Dallin H. Oaks, "Faith in the Lord Jesus Christ,'" *Ensign*, May 1994, 98–100.)

GOSPEL ART

Building the Ark, 7
Esther, 21
Jesus Calms the Storm, 40
Christ Walking on the Water, 43

Jesus Shows His Wounds, 60
Enos Praying, 72
Abinadi before King Noah, 75
Alma Baptizes in the Waters of Mormon, 76
Two Thousand Young Warriors, 80
Joseph Smith Seeks Wisdom in the Bible, 89
The First Vision, 90
Young Man Being Baptized –103
Girl Being Baptized, 104
Abraham Taking Isaac to Be Sacrificed, 105
Three Men in the Fiery Furnace, 116
Daniel in the Lions' Den, 117
Moses and the Brass Serpent, 123
Christ Healing a Blind Man, 213
Jesus Blessing Jairus's Daughter, 215
Christ and the Children, 216
The Liahona, 302
The Anti-Nephi-Lehies Burying Their Swords, 311
The Brother of Jared Sees the Finger of the Lord, 318

VIDEOS

"By Faith": https://www.lds.org/media-library/video/2016-03-018-by-faith
"Our Faith": https://www.lds.org/media-library/video/missionary/our-faith
"Faith": https://www.lds.org/media-library/video/topics/faith
"Light Switch": https://www.lds.org/media-library/video/2015-06-023-light-switch?category=topics/faith
"Faith and Works": https://www.lds.org/media-library/video/2012-06-2060-faith-and-works?category=topics/faith
"Faith and Trials": https://www.lds.org/media-library/video/2011-03-086-faith-and-trials?category=topics/faith
"A Test of Faith": https://www.lds.org/media-library/video/2012-06-1240-a-test-of-faith?category=topics/faith

OBJECT LESSONS

↱ Put clear vinegar in a clear glass so the class members think it is filled with water. Ask the class what you could do to make the "water" overflow. Ask them to do it with their minds by thinking very hard. Did that make any change? (No.) Add some baking soda, and the vinegar will immediately begin to bubble up. Relate this to how we need to take action. When we act, our faith has more power!

↝ Ask for volunteers to come to the front of the class one at a time for an activity similar to charades. Invite people to act out certain acts of faith from the Bible. Allow them to choose a three-by-five-inch index card that has a faith-filled moment written on it, such as Noah building the ark, Moses parting the Red Sea, Daniel surviving the den of lions, and David standing up against Goliath. It should be pretty entertaining. Now invite more people to come up to the front of the class to act out modern-day faith. You could allow them to create their own examples or give them three-by-five-inch index cards that list things like turning off a computer when a pornographic site pops up, paying tithing, attending the temple, reading the scriptures, etc.

↝ Display two flowers in two vases of water, one flower being fake and the other real. Ask the class to describe the difference. The fake one is "dead," although it may look nice. The real one is alive, has a beautiful aroma, and is pleasant to the touch. We become alive when our faith is alive and growing. Create your "sanctuary of faith" with living faith in the living Christ.

ARTICLES

Devin G. Durrant, "Teaching in the Home—a Joyful and Sacred Responsibility," *Ensign*, May 2018.

Carol B. Thomas, "Strengthen Home and Family," *Ensign*, May 2002.

Spencer W. Kimball, "Strengthening the Family—the Basic Unit of the Church," *Ensign*, May 1978.

Neil L. Andersen, "Faith Is Not by Chance, but by Choice," *Ensign*, Nov. 2015.

Richard G. Scott, "Make the Exercise of Faith Your First Priority," *Ensign*, Nov. 2014.

Russell M. Nelson, "Face the Future with Faith," *Ensign*, May 2011.

Russell M. Nelson, "Let Your Faith Show," *Ensign*, May 2014.

James E. Faust, "The Shield of Faith," *Ensign*, May 2000.

CHALLENGE

Write a list of all the gospel principles you know to be true, and write how you came to that knowledge and understanding. This will be the beginning of a wonderful testimony journal! When your faith weakens due to trials or sorrow, you will be able to return to your journal and be uplifted and strengthened.

• •

DOCTRINAL MASTERY PASSAGES

Book of Mormon
1 Nephi 3:7
Mosiah 4:30
Alma 32:21
Ether 12:6
Ether 12:27
Moroni 7:45
Moroni 10:4–5

Old Testament
Proverbs 3:5–6

New Testament
Matthew 5:14–16
Romans 1:16
1 Corinthians 10:13
Ephesians 4:11–14
James 2:17–18

Doctrine and Covenants
D&C 1:37–38
D&C 84:33–39

Joseph Smith—History
JS—H 1:15–20

• •

PREACH MY GOSPEL

Pages 18, 22, 38, 61, 90–102, 115, 116, 155

• •

NOTES

_____

_____

_____

_____

_____

_____

Lesson 8

COMMITMENT TO COMMANDMENTS

. . . .

MUSIC

"Keep the Commandments," *Hymns*, no. 303
"Dare to Do Right," *Children's Songbook*, 158
"I Will Be Valiant," *Children's Songbook*, 162
"How Gentle God's Commands," *Hymns*, no. 125
"Stand for the Right," *Children's Songbook*, 159

. . . .

SUMMARY

In the October 2018 general conference, President Henry B. Eyring encouraged us to "try, try, try." He said, "Our mortal life is designed by a loving God to be a test and source of growth for each of us" ("Try, Try, Try," *Ensign*, Nov. 2018). We can show our commitment to God by keeping His commandments.

Most of us would say that we love God. How do we show Him our sincere love and gratitude? The answer is simple: by doing His will and keeping His commandments (see John 14:15). We are commanded to love God and our fellow man. The order of those mandates is significant. If we truly love God, everything else will fall into place in its proper order. The blessings we receive by loving God will help us to love and bless our fellow man.

God desires to bless us, so He makes covenants with us. His promises are sure if we keep our commitments. He shows us that when we obey certain laws of heaven, we receive specific blessings (see D&C 130:21). He is our loving Heavenly Father, who formed this earth as a school for our learning and progression. We need to believe in God but also DO His will, despite what others do. We are not only His greatest creation, but we are His sons and daughters. By committing to His commandments and serving others, we can become like Him and return to live with Him.

• •

QUOTES

- "Let us seek to be totally committed. Then we will not fall upon stony places, wither away, or stray from the paths of security and happiness. Those who serve with complete dedication wherever called do not wilt, wither, wonder, or wander. Their roots are deep and solidly planted in the fertile soils of the kingdom." (Marvin J. Ashton, "Who Will Forfeit the Harvest?" *Ensign*, Nov. 1978.)
- "True happiness is not made in getting something. True happiness is becoming something. This can be done by being committed to lofty goals. We cannot become something without commitment." (Marvin J. Ashton, "'The Word Is Commitment,'" *Ensign*, Nov. 1983.)
- "Love is the measure of our faith, the inspiration for our obedience, and the true altitude of our discipleship." (Dieter F. Uchtdorf, "The Love of God," *Ensign*, Nov. 2009.)
- "To love God with all your heart, soul, mind, and strength is all-consuming and all-encompassing. It is no lukewarm endeavor. It is total commitment of our very being—physically, mentally, emotionally, and spiritually—to a love of the Lord." (Ezra Taft Benson, "The Great Commandment—Love the Lord," *Ensign*, May 1988.)
- "We have got to reach a higher plane: we have got to love God more than we love the world." (Lorenzo Snow, "Chapter 21: Loving God More Than We Love the World," *Teachings of Presidents of the Church: Lorenzo Snow*, 2011.)

• •

GOSPEL ART

Building the Ark, 7
Boy Samuel Called by the Lord, 18
Daniel Refusing the King's Meat and Wine, 23
Three Men in the Fiery Furnace, 25
Daniel in the Lions' Den, 26
John the Baptist Baptizing Jesus, 35)
Calling of the Fishermen, 37

VIDEOS

"Why Does God Give Us Commandments?": https://www.lds.org/media-library/video/2015-01-014-why-does-god-give-us-commandments
"Commandments": https://www.lds.org/media-library/video/topics/commandments
"Obedience Brings Blessings": https://www.lds.org/media-library/video/2014-06-1130-obedience-brings-blessings
"The Two Great Commandments": https://www.lds.org/media-library/video/2013-10-1160-the-two-great-commandments
"Obedience": https://www.lds.org/media-library/video/2011-03-075-obedience
"The Greatest Commandment": http://www.lds.org/media-library/video/2011-10-052-the-greatest-commandment

OBJECT LESSONS

- Show the class a pen. Tell a volunteer to try to take pen. When they grab it, say "No, don't DO it. You were supposed to just TRY." Commitment means we're all in. The Lord takes our commitment seriously. We know He will always keep His end of the bargain, and He expects us to do the same.
- Scramble up the letters to words using this fun online tool: www.superkids.com/aweb/tools/words/scramble/. Try words like *oancdmemstmn* (commandments) or *ipisoetrir* (priorities). Have the class try to unscramble the words.
- Invite the class to sing "I Am a Child of God," and then tell them the story behind the words. Originally the words read, "Teach me all that I must *know* to live with Him someday," but President Spencer W. Kimball said that that's not enough—we have to *do*. Keeping the commandments isn't just learning about them; it is actually doing them.

ARTICLES

John B. Dickson, "Commitment to the Lord," *Ensign*, May 2007.

Carole M. Stephens, "'If Ye Love Me, Keep My Commandments,'" *Ensign*, Nov. 2015.

Thomas S. Monson, "Keep the Commandments," *Ensign*, Nov. 2015.

Howard W. Hunter, "Commitment to God," *Ensign*, Nov. 1982.

David B. Haight, "Live the Commandments," *Ensign*, May 1998.

Von G. Keetch, "Blessed and Happy Are Those Who Keep the Commandments of God," *Ensign*, Nov. 2015.

Bruce A. Carlson, "When the Lord Commands," *Ensign*, May 2010.

• •

CHALLENGE

Create a to-do list of things you need to accomplish this week. Put them into two categories: *Ways I show that I love God* and *Ways I show that I love others.* Notice how many fit in neither category. Where are you spending the majority of your time and energy? Write a list of ways you can show that you are more committed to keeping those two great commandments.

• •

DOCTRINAL MASTERY PASSAGES

Book of Mormon
1 Nephi 3:7
1 Nephi 19:23
2 Nephi 32:3
Jacob 2:18–19
Helaman 5:12
Moroni 7:16–17
Moroni 10:4–5

Old Testament
Exodus 20:3–17
Deuteronomy 7:3–4
Joshua 24:15
Job 19:25–26

Proverbs 3:5–6
Daniel 2:44–45

New Testament
Matthew 6:24
John 7:17
John 14:15
John 17:3
2 Thessalonians 2:1–3

Doctrine and Covenants
D&C 14:7
D&C 19:16–19
D&C 130:20–21

• •

PREACH MY GOSPEL

Pages 5, 7, 31–32, 37, 48, 66, 72, 76

· ·

NOTES

Lesson 9

FOLLOW THE
LIVING PROPHET

MUSIC

"Come, Listen to a Prophet's Voice," *Hymns*, no. 21
"God Bless Our Prophet Dear," *Hymns*, no. 24
"Praise to the Man," *Hymns*, no. 27
"We Thank Thee, O God, for a Prophet," *Hymns*, no. 19

SUMMARY

The First Counselor in the Presiding Bishopric, Bishop Dean M. Davies, encouraged us in the October 2018 general conference to listen to the prophet's voice. He counseled, "As we solidify in our lives the practice of listening to and heeding the voice of the living prophets, we will reap eternal blessings" ("Come, Listen to a Prophet's Voice," *Ensign*, Nov. 2018). We have seen the Lord work through our living prophet, President Russell M. Nelson, as new changes in the Church have created growth, strength, and excitement!

God communicates to His people through a living prophet, a man called through priesthood authority to represent Him. The prophet is also the President of The Church of Jesus Christ of Latter-day Saints and holds the keys of the kingdom on earth. The prophet receives revelation for the Church and leads the administration of priesthood ordinances. He is also called a seer and revelator. By following the Lord's chosen mouthpiece, we will never be led astray.

When we sustain the prophet by the show of our raised hands in church, we are not voting for him; we are affirming our support and commitment to follow the Lord's anointed mouthpiece on earth.

QUOTES

↪ "A prophet . . . is the authorized representative of the Lord. While the world may not recognize him, the important requirement is that God speaks through him." (A. Theodore Tuttle, "What Is a Living Prophet?" *Ensign*, July 1973, 18–20.)

↪ "Our sustaining support of prophets, seers, and revelators is not in the upraised hand alone, but more so in our courage, testimony, and faith to listen to, heed, and follow them." (Dennis B. Neuenschwander, "Living Prophets, Seers, and Revelators," *Liahona*, Jan. 2001, 49–51; or *Ensign*, Nov. 2000, 40–42.)

↪ "When we sustain, it means we *do* something about our belief. Our testimony of the prophet turns into action when we sustain him." (Janette Hales Beckham, "Sustaining the Living Prophets," *Ensign*, May 1996, 84–85.)

↪ "Surely one of the crowning blessings of membership in this Church is the blessing of being led by living prophets of God." (Kevin R. Duncan, "Our Very Survival," *Ensign*, Nov. 2010.)

↪ "Prophets often raise a voice of warning but also provide steady, pragmatic counsel to help us weather the storms of life." (Steven E. Snow, "Get On with Our Lives," *Ensign*, May 2009.)

GOSPEL ART

Building the Ark, 7
Abraham Taking Isaac to be Sacrificed, 9
Moses and the Burning Bush, 13
Boy Samuel Called by the Lord, 18
Lehi Prophesying to the People of Jerusalem, 67
Enos Praying, 72
King Benjamin Addresses His People, 74
Abinadi before King Noah, 75
Samuel the Lamanite on the Wall, 81
The Prophet Joseph Smith, 122
Latter-day Prophets, 122–137

VIDEOS

"Prophets and Revelation: Hearing His Voice": https://www.lds.org/media
-library/video/2012-10-005-prophets-and-revelation-hearing-his-voice
?category=youth-curriculum/may-prophets-and-revelation

"Follow the Prophet": https://www.lds.org/manual/preach-my-gospel/asl/chap
ter3/lesson4

"Life's Greatest Decisions": https://www.lds.org/media-library/video/2003
-09-04-lifes-greatest-decisions

"We Need Living Prophets": https://www.lds.org/media-library/video/2012
-04-15-we-need-living-prophets

"A Steady, Reassuring Voice": https://www.lds.org/media-library/video/2012
-08-3150-a-steady-reassuring-voice

"Testimonies from Prophets and Apostles": https://www.lds.org/media-library
/video/prophets-and-apostles/prophets-and-apostles-sub-category

OBJECT LESSONS

🔹 Invite a few volunteers to come up to the front of the room and tape down their thumbs to the palms of their hands. Ask them to do some simple tasks, such as tying their shoes, buttoning a shirt, or using a knife and fork to cut a piece of bread. Explain that without a prophet, we don't have all of the information or tools to live the gospel in its fulness.

🔹 Invite the class members to sign a birthday card for the prophet. You can find out his birthday at www.lds.org.

🔹 Tell the class you are going to re-enact one of the miracles that a prophet of God performed: parting the Red Sea. Put a few drops of red dye in some water on a saucer. Next, pour a few drops of rubbing alcohol onto the saucer with an eyedropper. Don't tell the class that rubbing alcohol is in the dropper. The rubbing alcohol will actually make a little dry spot on the saucer! Ask the class if this experiment reminded them of any story in the Bible. As they talk about Moses and the parting of the Red Sea, the conversation can then be guided toward the importance of prophets to lead us and guide us. Ask the class what kinds of miracles our latter-day prophets have performed. They may not be things as dramatic as parting the Red Sea, but they are just as powerful. Miracles could include the building of temples, humanitarian aid, changes in programs that bring us closer to Christ (ministering, home centered Sundays, etc.), and so on.

🔹 Gift-wrap two boxes—one empty box and one box filled with treats. Tell the class that one of the boxes has something special in it while the other one has nothing. Ask a volunteer to choose a box. Let the volunteer see what's inside the box, and then ask the class if they want the volunteer to decide for them. Of course, they'll say yes because he or she now knows what's in both boxes. We follow the prophet because he has "seen what's in the box" of life! He knows what choices we need to make in order to receive eternal rewards.

ARTICLES

Dean M. Davies, "Come, Listen to a Prophet's Voice," *Ensign*, Nov. 2018.
Russell M. Nelson, "Sustaining the Prophets," *Ensign*, Nov. 2014.
Neil L. Andersen, "The Prophet of God," *Ensign*, May 2018.
F. Michael Watson, "His Servants, the Prophets," *Ensign*, May 2009.
David B. Haight, "A Prophet Chosen of the Lord," *Ensign*, May 1986.
Jeffrey R. Holland, "'My Words . . . Never Cease,'" *Ensign*, May 2008.
Jeffrey R. Holland, "Prophets in the Land Again," *Ensign*, Nov. 2006.
Dieter F. Uchtdorf, "Heeding the Voice of the Prophets," *Ensign*, July 2008.
Gordon B. Hinckley, "'We Thank Thee, O God, for a Prophet,'" *Ensign*, Sept. 1991.

CHALLENGE

Read talks from the most recent general conference to hear what our current prophet has counseled us to do. Make a list of the things you need to work on in your life in order to be able to say you are following the prophet.

DOCTRINAL MASTERY PASSAGES

Book of Mormon
1 Nephi 3:7
Alma 37:6–7
3 Nephi 27:27

Old Testament
Abraham 3:22–23
Exodus 33:11

Jeremiah 16:16
Daniel 2:44–45

New Testament
Matthew 16:15–19
Ephesians 4:11–14

Doctrine and Covenants
D&C 84:33–39

PREACH MY GOSPEL

Pages 7, 35–36, 44–45, 66, 75, 88

. . . .

NOTES

_____

_____

_____

_____

_____

_____

_____

_____

_____

_____

_____

_____

_____

_____

_____

_____

_____

_____

_____

_____

_____

_____

_____

Lesson 10

STRENGTHENING INDIVIDUALS AND FAMILIES

. . . .

MUSIC

"Families Can Be Together Forever," *Hymns*, no. 300
"Father, Cheer Our Souls Tonight," *Hymns*, no. 231
"From Homes of Saints Glad Songs Arise," *Hymns*, no. 297
"Home Can Be a Heaven on Earth," *Hymns*, no. 298
"Love at Home," *Hymns*, no. 294
"Our Mountain Home So Dear," *Hymns*, no. 33
"Teach Me to Walk in the Light," *Hymns*, no. 304
"The Lord Be with Us," *Hymns*, no. 161

. . . .

SUMMARY

Elder Steven R. Bangerter gave an excellent talk in the October 2018 general conference entitled "Laying the Foundation of a Great Work" to encourage us to strengthen individuals and families. He said, "Consistent, wholesome family traditions that include prayer, scripture reading, family home evening, and attendance at Church meetings, though seemingly small and simple, create a culture of love, respect, unity, and security" (*Ensign*, Nov. 2018).

Life is eternal. We come from heavenly parents who are waiting for us to return to them, having learned the lessons of life and gained the characteristics they possess. To remind us of our heavenly home, we are given the opportunity to be parents here on earth and raise a family of our own. Salvation is a family affair. We are placed here as families to learn how to care for one another so that we may all safely return home together. Temple marriage is a covenant partnership with the Lord that allows us to seal souls together as eternal families.

• •

QUOTES

➵ "Our family is the focus of our greatest work and joy in this life; so will it be throughout all eternity." (Russell M. Nelson, "'Set in Order Thy House,'" *Liahona*, Jan. 2002, 80–83.)

➵ "The key to strengthening our families is having the Spirit of the Lord come into our homes. The goal of our families is to be on the strait and narrow path." (Robert D. Hales, "Strengthening Families: Our Sacred Duty," *Liahona*, July 1999, 37–40.)

➵ "The family unit is fundamental not only to society and to the Church but also to our hope for eternal life." (Henry B. Eyring, "The Family," *Liahona*, Oct. 1998, 12–23.)

➵ "The plan of the Father is that family love and companionship will continue into the eternities." (Robert D. Hales, "The Eternal Family," *Ensign*, Nov. 1996, 64–67.)

• •

GOSPEL ART

Adam and Eve Kneeling at an Altar, 4
Adam and Eve Teaching Their Children, 5
Jacob Blessing His Sons, 12
My Father's House, 52
Young Couple Going to the Temple, 120

• •

VIDEOS

"Strengthening Home and Family": https://www.lds.org/media-library/video/2014-02-0070-strengthening-home-and-family

"Strengthening Families": https://www.lds.org/media-library/video/2011-07-154-strengthening-families

"A New Vision": https://www.lds.org/media-library/video/hasten-the-work/a-new-vision

"Strengthen Thy Brethren": https://www.lds.org/media-library/video/2011-12-18-strengthen-thy-brethren?category=annual-mutual-theme/2012-arise-and-shine-forth

"Arise and Shine Forth": https://www.lds.org/media-library/video/2011-12 -20-arise?category=annual-mutual-theme/2012-arise-and-shine-forth

OBJECT LESSONS

- Pass out sheets of paper that have five columns on them with the following labels: Our family motto, Family goals for this year, Family accomplishments from last year, Family service projects, and Family talents. Encourage class members to write down the answers to those questions and take the paper home to continue filling it out with their family.
- Invite people to come to class prepared to share fun family traditions they have year round and during holidays.
- Pass out copies of the "The Family: A Proclamation to the World" to everyone in the class, and have them color and decorate them during your lesson.

ARTICLES

Jeffrey R. Holland, "'Be With and Strengthen Them,'" *Ensign*, May 2018.
Mary N. Cook, "Strengthen Home and Family," *Ensign*, Nov. 2007.
Robert D. Hales, "The Eternal Family," *Ensign*, Nov. 1996, 64–67.
Henry B. Eyring, "The Family," *Ensign*, Feb. 1998, 10–18.
Russell M. Nelson, "'Set in Order Thy House,'" *Ensign*, Nov. 2001, 69–71.
L. Tom Perry, "The Importance of the Family," *Ensign*, May 2003, 40–43.

CHALLENGE

No family is perfect. Our love for each other deepens when we focus on the good and the future rather than the bad and the past. Write a list of some of the positive qualities each member of your family has. You will begin to see them as the Lord sees them. Now write down their goals that you know of. Consider what things you could do to help them achieve their goals.

DOCTRINAL MASTERY PASSAGES

Book of Mormon
2 Nephi 2:27

2 Nephi 32:8–9
Mosiah 3:19

Mosiah 4:30
Alma 32:21
Alma 37:35
Moroni 10:4–5

Old Testament
Deuteronomy 7:3–4

Joshua 1:8
Daniel 2:44–45

New Testament
John 17:3

Doctrine and Covenants
D&C 14:7

• •

PREACH MY GOSPEL

Pages 3, 18, 19, 22, 25, 30, 31, 32, 33, 38, 90–102, 213, 214

• •

NOTES

_____

_____

_____

_____

_____

_____

_____

_____

_____

_____

_____

_____

_____

_____

Lesson 11

A Holier Approach to Caring and Ministering

· ·

MUSIC

"Because I Have Been Given Much," *Hymns*, no. 219
"Love One Another," *Hymns*, no. 308
"'Tis Sweet to Sing the Matchless Love," *Hymns*, no. 177
"Truth Reflects upon Our Senses," *Hymns*, no. 273
"We Have Partaken of Thy Love," *Hymns*, no. 155

· ·

SUMMARY

Sister Bonnie H. Cordon shared a sweet message about becoming a shepherd during the October 2018 general conference. To help us improve our ministering efforts, she reminded us of our divine mandate: "We have been assigned specific individuals and families to tend so we are certain that all of the Lord's flock are accounted for and no one is forgotten. Numbering, however, is not really about numbers; it is about making certain *each* person feels the love of the Savior through someone who serves *for* Him. In that way, all can recognize that they are known by a loving Father in Heaven" ("Becoming a Shepherd," *Ensign*, Nov. 2018).

As we learn to transition from the home teaching and visiting teaching programs to the new ministering program, we are learning how to serve and minister more like Christ did. Our visits with the people we are assignment to are less about giving a formal lesson and more about being sensitive to their unique needs and serving in ways that ease their burdens, build their faith, and lift their spirits.

. . . .

QUOTES

➳ "We will minister in His name, with His power and authority, and with His loving-kindness." (Russell M. Nelson, "Ministering with the Power and Authority of God," *Ensign*, May 2018.)

➳ "Through a lifetime of service in this Church, I have learned that it really doesn't matter *where* one serves. What the Lord cares about is *how* one serves." (Russell M. Nelson, "Ministering with the Power and Authority of God," *Ensign*, May 2018.)

➳ "I pray that you wonderful young men will not only be worthy to *receive* ministering angels, but that you . . . will *become* a ministering angel in the lives of others." (Spencer J. Condie, "Becoming a Great Benefit to Our Fellow Beings," *Ensign*, May 2002.)

➳ "May we show our gratitude and love for God by ministering with love to our eternal sisters and brothers." (Jean B. Bingham, "Ministering as the Savior Does," *Ensign*, May 2018.)

➳ "As you love His children, Heavenly Father will guide you, and angels will assist you. You will be given power to bless lives and rescue souls." (David L. Beck, "Your Sacred Duty to Minister," *Ensign*, May 2013.)

. . . .

GOSPEL ART

Ruth Gleaning in the Fields, 17
The Sermon on the Mount, 39
Jesus Blessing Jairus's Daughter, 41
Christ Healing the Sick at Bethesda, 42
The Good Samaritan, 42
Jesus Washing the Apostles' Feet, 55
King Benjamin Addresses His People, 74
Alma Baptizes in the Waters of Mormon, 76

. . . .

VIDEOS

"Ministering with the Power and Authority of God": https://www.lds.org/general-conference/2018/04/ministering-with-the-power-and-authority-of-god

"Ministering as the Savior Does": https://www.lds.org/general-conference /2018/04/ministering-as-the-savior-does

"Why We Minister": https://www.lds.org/media-library/video/2018-04-0030 -why-we-minister

"Ministering to the Needs of Members": https://www.lds.org/general-confer ence/1980/10/ministering-to-the-needs-of-members

"Love Thy Neighbor": http://www.youtube.com/watch?v=lq5IzDW4ufA

OBJECT LESSONS

- Ask someone to fold a fitted bed sheet without help. Next, ask two people to do the same task. Tasks are often easier when you have someone to help you, including living the gospel! Invite the class to share experiences when they helped their ministering families with household tasks while they got to know each other.

- Play some ice-breaker games to give the class examples of things they can do to get to know their ministering families better. You can find a terrific list of fun ideas at https://www.icebreakers.ws/.

- Hand each person a piece of sand paper and a little wooden heart. Ask them to rub off the edges to get rid of the roughness and slivers. Talk about how the Lord knows that our rough edges will be smoothed as we learn to serve others. We truly become more like Him as we "feed His sheep." Invite the class to decorate the hearts with colored markers or paint while you teach the rest of the lesson. They can give both the wooden heart and their real heart to their ministering families on their next visit!

- While teaching your lesson, remove your jacket, belt, and shoes and unbutton some buttons on your sleeves, all without explaining why. At the end, say, "You probably won't remember a word I said by the time you get home, but you will never forget what I did. Actions speak louder than words."

- Pass around a mirror, and ask the class to look in it. Ask them when they focused on their own image if they were able to see anyone else? (No.) By serving others, we focus less on our own problems and challenges and gain improved perspective.

ARTICLES

Jean B. Bingham, "Ministering as the Savior Does," *Ensign*, May 2018.

Russell M. Nelson, "Ministering with the Power and Authority of God," *Ensign*, May 2018.

Henry B. Eyring, "Inspired Ministering," *Ensign*, May 2018.

Robert J. Matthews, "What 'Loving Your Neighbor' Really Means," *Ensign*, Oct. 1975.

James M. Paramore, "'They Taught and Did Minister One to Another,'" *Ensign*, May 1986.

Thomas S. Monson, "How Do We Show Our Love?" *Ensign*, Jan. 1998.

Robert J. Whetten, "A Real Neighbor," *Liahona*, May 2005.

CHALLENGE

Think of the people you have been called to minister to. Write a list of all the things you have in common with them. Jot down things you know they like or don't like. "Friend" them on social media, or send them a cheerful text. Begin a list of things you could do for them. Prayerfully consider their needs and how you could be a blessing in their lives.

DOCTRINAL MASTERY PASSAGES

Book of Mormon
1 Nephi 3:7
Jacob 2:18–19
Mosiah 2:17
Mosiah 4:30
Moroni 7:45

Old Testament
Leviticus 19:18

New Testament
Matthew 5:14–16
Matthew 25:40

Doctrine and Covenants
D&C 84:33–39
D&C 137:7–10

PREACH MY GOSPEL

Pages 2, 8, 62, 87, 115, 118, 123–126, 168–169

NOTES

_____

_____

_____

_____

_____

_____

_____

_____

_____

_____

_____

_____

_____

_____

_____

_____

_____

_____

Lesson 12

LEARNING THROUGH TRIALS AND PAIN

MUSIC

"Cast Thy Burden upon the Lord," *Hymns,* no. 110
"I Need My Heavenly Father," *Children's Songbook,* 18
"Arise, O Glorious Zion," *Hymns,* no. 40
"Awake, Ye Saints of God, Awake!" *Hymns,* no. 17

SUMMARY

At the October 2018 general conference, Brother M. Joseph Brough talked about how trials and pain can teach us if we are humble and willing to learn. He gave us this wise counsel: "To help us travel and triumph over our hard times with such glimpses of eternity, may I suggest two things. We must face hard things, first, by forgiving others and, second, by giving ourselves to Heavenly Father" ("Lift Up Your Head and Rejoice," *Ensign,* Nov. 2018).

Wickedness is increasing at an ever-quickening pace, and our homes and values are being assaulted on every side. The trials and tribulations we face will help refine us as we grow spiritually and build our Christlike character. Adversity is designed to be a part of our earthly life experience, so rather than question, "Why me?" we should ask, "What can I learn from this experience?"

One of the purposes of mortality is to show which choices we'll make, so there must be opposition in all things in order for us to exercise agency. Our trials are designed to soften our hearts and bring us closer to Christ. We need not fear nor lose hope. Sometimes we bring suffering on ourselves due to poor decisions, but other times we have no control over the actions of others. Either way, following the Savior will ease our burdens and lighten our loads. He has overcome the world and wants to help us do the same.

• •

QUOTES

➤ "Repeated assurances have been given regarding the benefits and blessings of positive responses to adversity, however undeserved. The witness of the Spirit and the manifestation of greater things often follow the trial of one's faith. Spiritual refinement may be realized in the furnace of affliction. Thereby we may be prepared to experience personal and direct contact with God." (Ronald E. Poelman, "Adversity and the Divine Purpose of Mortality," *Ensign*, May 1989.)

➤ "Rather than simply passing through trials, we must allow trials to pass through us in ways that sanctify us." (Neal A. Maxwell, "Enduring Well," *Ensign*, Apr. 1999.)

➤ "Paul, in describing our 'perilous times,' did not promise that things would necessarily get easier or necessarily better. He did give counsel to those seeking comfort and assurance in the face of the deteriorating conditions of our day. Just as his prophecies or predictions were clearly accurate, so is his direction to us remarkably relevant as well. Said he, 'Continue . . . in the things which thou hast learned and hast been assured of, knowing of whom thou hast learned them.'" (Cecil O. Samuelson Jr., "Perilous Times," *Ensign*, Nov. 2004.)

➤ "These are the last days. As has been foretold by God's holy prophets since the world began, they are challenging times, and they are going to become even more challenging. . . . [Satan's] sole purpose is to make you and me as miserable as he is, and the best way for him to accomplish that is to entice us into disobedience. Although there are all kinds of misery in this world, the only kind that is eternal is misery of the soul. And that kind of misery is centered in sin and transgression." (M. Russell Ballard, "'When Shall These Things Be?'" *Ensign*, Dec. 1996.)

• •

GOSPEL ART

Building the Ark, 7
Ruth Gleaning in the Fields, 17
Three Men in the Fiery Furnace, 25
Daniel in the Lions' Den, 26

• •

VIDEOS

"Trial of Adversity": https://www.lds.org/media-library/video/2011-04-002
-trial-of-adversity

"Comfort in Trials": https://www.lds.org/media-library/video/2012-01-002
-comfort-in-trials

"That We Might Not Shrink": https://www.lds.org/media-library/video/2013
-03-0020-that-we-might-not--shrink-dc-1918?category=topics/adversity

"Be Not Troubled": http://lds.org/library/display/0,4945,6635-1-4786-3,00.
html

"Trials and Adversity": Julie Beck: http://mormonchannel.org/relief-society
/questions-and-answers/10

"Enduring It Well": Shauna Ewing: http://mormonchannel.org/enduring
-it-well/61-shauna-ewing-compassion-upon-you-part-2

"Come What May, and Love It": https://www.lds.org/media-library/video
/2009-01-03-come-what-may-and-love-it

• •

OBJECT LESSONS

➥ Bring a backpack and some rocks. Pass out pieces of paper, and invite the
class to write down a challenge or trial that they have faced in the past
or are currently facing. Wrap each piece of paper around a different rock
and put them in the backpack. Invite someone to carry the backpack
around the room. Carefully, take a rock out of the backpack and read the
trial. Ask the class how the Lord could provide help for that particular
challenge. (Possible answers: loving parents, helpful friends, a prophet,
scriptures, a healthy body, prayer, modern technology, Church programs,
etc.) Do the same with each of the other rocks, each time removing the
rock but returning the paper to the backpack. In the end, the backpack

should still have the papers inside, but no rocks. The Lord allows us to go through trials to build our spiritual muscles, all the while removing the heavy burden.

↦ Decorate the classroom with kites. Invite the class to compare our lives to that of a kite. (Possible answers: our trials are like the wind that pushes us around, yet also allows us to fly; the string is like the gospel, which helps control the direction of our lives and anchor us; etc.)

↦ Show two empty water bottles to the class. On a glove, write the word "Trials." Write the word "Faith" on the lid of the water bottles. Take the lid off of one of the water bottles, and ask what happens when trials come along in our life and we don't have faith to withstand them. Invite someone to wear the glove and try to crush the bottle with no lid. It's easy to do. Next, invite the volunteer to try to crush the water bottle with the lid still on. It should be much harder to do. The lesson should illustrate that we can endure trials much better when we have faith that the Lord is still with us and that there is a purpose in our suffering.

• •

ARTICLES

Thomas S. Monson, "Tears, Trials, Trust, Testimony," *Ensign*, May 1987.
Anne Marie Rose, "Facing Trials with Optimism," *Ensign*, May 1996.
Bruce R. McConkie, "The Coming Tests and Trials of Glory," *Ensign*, May 1980.
Richard G. Scott, "The Sustaining Power of Faith in Times of Uncertainty and Testing," *Ensign*, May 2003.
Cecil O. Samuelson Jr., "Perilous Times," *Liahona*, Nov. 2004.
Boyd K. Packer, "The Test," *Liahona*, Nov. 2008.
Neal A. Maxwell, "Enduring Well," *Ensign*, Apr. 1997.

• •

CHALLENGE

Each day is filled with challenges and problems to overcome. Sometimes we create our own problems by making bad choices, but often we are placed in difficult circumstances because of other reasons not of our own doing. Write a list of the trials in your life and the Christlike qualities you can develop as you endure and overcome them.

• •

DOCTRINAL MASTERY PASSAGES

Book of Mormon
1 Nephi 3:7
2 Nephi 2:27
2 Nephi 28:7–9
Jacob 2:18–19
Mosiah 3:19
Mosiah 4:30
Alma 34:32–34
Alma 41:10
Helaman 5:12
Moroni 7:16–17
Moroni 7:45

Old Testament
Exodus 20:3–17
Joshua 1:8
Isaiah 1:18

New Testament
Matthew 6:24
John 7:17
John 14:15
1 Corinthians 10:13
Revelation 20:12–13

Doctrine and Covenants
D&C 1:37–38
D&C 14:7
D&C 58:26–27

• •

PREACH MY GOSPEL

Pages 47–49, 66, 72, 75, 88, 150–151

• •

NOTES

_____

_____

_____

_____

_____

_____

_____

_____

Lesson 13

FORGIVENESS AND HEALING OLD WOUNDS

MUSIC

"Help Me, Dear Father," *Children's Songbook,* 99
"In Humility, Our Savior," *Hymns,* no. 172
"Nay, Speak No Ill," *Hymns,* no. 233
"Reverently and Meekly Now," *Hymns,* no. 185
"Lord, I Would Follow Thee," *Hymns,* no. 220

SUMMARY

Elder Neil L. Andersen spoke at the October 2018 general conference about forgiveness and healing old wounds. He reassured us, "In the crucible of earthly trials, patiently move forward, and the Savior's healing power will bring you light, understanding, peace, and hope" ("Wounded," *Ensign,* Nov. 2018).

We often pray that the Lord will forgive us for our weaknesses and transgressions, while at the same time we hold grudges against others who have wronged us. When we truly understand the gospel of Jesus Christ, we love one another and forgive each other. When we feel anger, bitterness, or hatred toward another person, we will not be able to feel peace, happiness, or the Spirit of the Lord. When we show forgiveness to someone who has wronged us, we are also showing Heavenly Father our gratitude for forgiving us of our transgressions and thanking Him for the Atonement, which allows us to repent and be clean once again.

Some people leave the Church because they have been offended or hurt by some of the members. Though they all know that we're imperfect people trying to improve, they chose to let their feelings toward those who caused the offence supersede the good actions of repentant people. We must be patient with each other and remember that the gospel is still true.

QUOTES

- "A spirit of forgiveness and an attitude of love and compassion toward those who may have wronged us is of the very essence of the gospel of Jesus Christ." (Gordon B. Hinckley, "'Of You It Is Required to Forgive,'" *Ensign*, June 1991.)
- "Forgiveness means that problems of the past no longer dictate our destinies, and we can focus on the future with God's love in our hearts." (David E. Sorensen, "Forgiveness Will Change Bitterness to Love," *Ensign*, May 2003.)
- "Forgiveness is a glorious, healing principle. We do not need to be a victim twice. We can forgive." (Elder Kevin R. Duncan, "The Healing Ointment of Forgiveness," *Ensign*, May 2016.)
- "If there be any within the sound of my voice who nurture in their hearts the poisonous brew of enmity toward another, I plead with you to ask the Lord for strength to forgive. This expression of desire will be of the very substance of your repentance." (Gordon B. Hinckley, "'Of You It Is Required to Forgive,'" *Ensign*, Nov. 1980.)

GOSPEL ART

The Sermon on the Mount, 39
Jesus Praying in Gethsemane, 56
The Crucifixion, 57
Jesus Shows His Wounds, 60
Nephi Subdues His Rebellious Brothers, 70
Joseph Smith in Liberty Jail, 97
Exodus from Nauvoo, February–May 1846, 99

VIDEOS

"Forgiveness: My Burden Was Made Light": https://www.lds.org/media-library/video/2010-07-14-forgiveness-my-burden-was-made-light

"The Healing Power of Forgiveness": https://www.lds.org/media-library /video/2013-10-1050-the-healing-power-of-forgiveness

"Healing": https://www.lds.org/media-library/video/topics/healing

"Repentance and Forgiveness": https://www.lds.org/media-library/video /topics/repentance-and-forgiveness

"Love—the Essence of the Gospel": https://www.lds.org/media-library /video/2014-04-0250-president-thomas-s-monson?category=topics /repentance-and-forgiveness

• •

OBJECT LESSONS

⌐• Pull some weeds out of your yard and display them for the class to see. Talk about how hard it is to get rid of them and how they can completely overtake a lawn if not removed early. Now show the class long strips of green crepe paper, and tell them they represent mean things people have said or done to us over the years. Drape a long piece of crepe paper over your shoulder with each example you give. Like the green weeds, the green crepe paper can weigh you down or cover you with bitterness if you left it. We should have that same aversion to allowing ourselves to be offended as we do to weeds in our yard. Being offended by someone's bad behavior or unkind words is a CHOICE.

⌐• Have everyone line up in different ways: by height, weight, age, birth month, etc. Emphasize how we are all different but we are progressing through life together, and that we need to be patient with one another as we make mistakes.

⌐• Ask who would like the piece of paper in your pocket. You'll likely find that not many people will be interested. Now show them a twenty-dollar bill, and ask the same question. Of course, everyone will be interested now! Ask them why the difference in enthusiasm, since the money is just a piece of paper? Tell them you think it must be because it's new. Crumple up the twenty-dollar bill, and ask who wants it now. Of course, everyone will still want it. Put a pencil mark on it, and say, "Now the bill isn't perfect, so I'm sure you won't want it." Of course, they still will. Tear off a tiny corner and again offer it, saying, "Now it is incomplete and imperfect, so I'm sure you won't want it." Of course, they're still interested. Ask them why they want it. They'll answer that it has value. Tell them you're going to make it even more valuable by putting it in an envelope. Ask how much it's worth now. (Twenty dollars still.) Put it in a fancy box, and ask how much the paper is worth now. (Twenty dollars still.) Explain that we're like that twenty-dollar bill: We have value no matter if we look perfect, are old and wrinkled, are scarred, or live in a fancy house. God doesn't love us more or less. In our dealings with imperfect people, we need to remember their true value.

→ Set out several big blocks or bulky items with signs on them labeled "Sin." Ask a volunteer to pick up as many as he or she can. Once the volunteer's arms are full, ask him or her to bend down and pick up a slip of paper on the floor labeled "Forgiveness." (It should be difficult for her to do.) Point out that when we are full of sin ourselves, it becomes more difficult to forgive others.

ARTICLES

Jeffrey R. Holland, "The Ministry of Reconciliation," *Ensign*, Nov. 2018.

Larry J. Echo Hawk, "Even as Christ Forgives You, So Also Do Ye," *Ensign*, May 2018.

David E. Sorensen, "Forgiveness Will Change Bitterness to Love," *Ensign*, May 2003.

Kevin R. Duncan, "The Healing Ointment of Forgiveness," *Ensign*, May 2016.

Theodore M. Burton, "To Forgive Is Divine," *Ensign*, May 1983.

Lynn G. Robbins, "Until Seventy Times Seven," *Ensign*, May 2018.

CHALLENGE

Draw a line down the middle of a piece of paper, and label one side *If I forgive* and the other side *If I don't forgive*. If someone has wronged you, write down the consequences of forgiving or not forgiving that person. Now, on the other side of the paper, write steps you will take to forgive that person.

DOCTRINAL MASTERY PASSAGES

Book of Mormon
2 Nephi 28:7–9
Mosiah 3:19
Alma 34:32–34
3 Nephi 11:29
3 Nephi 27:27

Ether 12:27

Old Testament
Leviticus 19:18
Isaiah 1:18
Isaiah 53:3–5

New Testament
Revelation 20:12–13

Doctrine and Covenants
D&C 18:10, 15–16
D&C 58:42–43
D&C 64:9–11

● ●

PREACH MY GOSPEL

Pages 187, 188

● ●

NOTES

_____

_____

_____

_____

_____

_____

_____

_____

_____

_____

_____

_____

_____

_____

_____

_____

_____

_____

Lesson 14

HONORING THE
LORD'S HOLY DAY

• •

MUSIC

"Sabbath Day," *Hymns*, no. 148
"Gently Raise the Sacred Strain," *Hymns*, no. 146
"We Meet, Dear Lord," *Hymns*, no. 151
"O Thou Kind and Gracious Father," *Hymns*, no. 150
"Welcome, Welcome, Sabbath Morning," *Hymns*, no. 280

• •

SUMMARY

When the announcement about the new "home-centered and Church supported" Sunday plan was made in the October 2018 general conference, Elder Quentin L. Cook explained how the plan would work. He confidently explained, "As individuals and families engage in family councils, family history, ministering, service, personal worship, and joyful family time, the Sabbath day will truly be a delight" ("Deep and Lasting Conversion to Heavenly Father and the Lord Jesus Christ," *Ensign*, Nov. 2018).

There is now a sixty-minute sacrament meeting, a ten-minute transition, and then a fifty-minute class that alternates weeks between Sunday School and the priesthood, Relief Society, Young Men, or Young Women classes. You can read Elder Cook's talk and the outline of the new Sunday schedule at https://www.lds.org/general-conference/2018/10/deep-and-lasting-conversion-to-heavenly-father-and-the-lord-jesus-christ.

God ordained the Sabbath to be kept holy and declared it to be a day of rest from our regular labors. The Sabbath occurs every seven days and is designed to direct our thoughts away from the world and instead toward the Lord. In the beginning, God consecrated the seventh day to represent God's day of rest after He created the world. After Christ's Resurrection, the first day of the week was honored as the Sabbath to commemorate His Resurrection and symbolize how it is the Savior who truly gives us rest. The Sabbath day is an opportunity to show the Lord that we put Him first in our lives. The fourth commandment helps us to remember our covenants and reevaluate our priorities and weekly activities.

There is no list of dos and don'ts. A helpful guideline in determining whether an activity is appropriate for the Sabbath is to simply ask the following questions: Will it help me draw closer to God? Does it show respect and love for the Savior? Will it inspire me and direct my thoughts to the Lord? The Sabbath day is an opportunity to show the Lord that we put Him first in our lives.

QUOTES

- "Now is the time to ask ourselves: Is the Sabbath a holy day or a holiday? Shall I worship the Lord or worship pleasures and recreation?" (Charles Didier, "The Sabbath—Holy Day or Holiday?" *Ensign*, Oct. 1994, 26–31.)
- "Observing the Sabbath is not a restriction but a protection and a source of strength." (D. Kelly Ogden, "Remember the Sabbath Day," *Liahona*, May 1998, 16–23; or *Ensign*, Apr. 1994, 46–51.)
- "Our observance of the Sabbath is an indication of the depth of our conversion and our willingness to keep sacred covenants." (Earl C. Tingey, "The Sabbath Day and Sunday Shopping," *Ensign*, May 1996, 10–12.)
- "There is a sure protection for ourselves and our children against the plague of our day. The key to that sure protection surprisingly can be found in Sabbath observance." (James E. Faust, "The Lord's Day," *Ensign*, Nov. 1991, 33–35.)

GOSPEL ART

The Lord Created All Things, 2
Adam and Eve Kneeling at an Altar, 4
Adam and Eve Teaching Their Children, 5
The Ten Commandments, 14
Esther, 21
Jesus Praying with His Mother, 33
Mary and Martha, 45

VIDEOS

"The Sabbath as a Sign": https://www.lds.org/media-library/video/2015-04
-1010-video-the-sabbath-as-a-sign-0021?category=sabbath-day-at-home

"The Sabbath as a Delight": https://www.lds.org/media-library/video/2015-10
-1005-video-the-sabbath-as-a-delight-820?category=sabbath-day-at-home

"Sabbath Day Observance at Home": https://www.lds.org/media-library
/video/2015-04-1009-video-sabbath-day-observance-at-home-0055
?category=sabbath-day-at-home

"Upon My Holy Day: Getting Closer to God": https://www.lds.org/media
-library/video/2016-10-0001-upon-my-holy-day-getting-closer-to-god
?category=sabbath-day-at-church

"Sunday Is a Special Day": https://www.lds.org/media-library/video/2016
-04-2000-saturday-is-a-special-day?category=sabbath-day-at-church

OBJECT LESSONS

- Tell the class that you're going to perform a magic act. Have a volunteer peel a banana and slice it. Then present the volunteer with another banana, and demonstrate that you can slice the banana without peeling it first, just as we can enjoy the Sabbath without laboring on Sunday, by simply preparing ahead of time. Wave your hand over the pre-sliced banana, and the volunteer will peel it and find that the banana has already been "magically" sliced into pieces. Prepare the banana long before your lesson by pushing a sewing needle into the banana through the peel, preferably on a brown spot so no one will notice. Push the needle through, but not all the way through the opposite side. With the needle in the banana, move the needle up and down a few times to cut the soft center but not the peel. Repeat the process all the way down the length of the banana, about every inch or so. The pinholes will leave small brown marks, so enter the needle from different sides of the banana.

- Ask for a volunteer to put some white sugar, representing the Sabbath day, into a clear glass. Now ask him or her to add some hot chocolate mix, representing the rest of the week, on top of the sugar. The class will see a definite line dividing the two colors. Now ask the student to mix them up together. The Lord asks us to set apart the Sabbath day to make it different from the rest of the week. The Sabbath day should look and feel different from the rest of our week.

- Display a battery-operated flashlight with a weak battery. Talk about how ineffective it is, and explain that when our spiritual batteries are recharged every week on the Sabbath, our eternal vision is brighter.

ARTICLES

Henry B. Eyring, "Gratitude on the Sabbath Day," *Ensign*, Nov. 2016.

Ezra Taft Benson, "Keeping the Sabbath Day Holy," *Ensign*, May 1971.

H. Aldridge Gillespie, "The Blessing of Keeping the Sabbath Day Holy," *Ensign*, Nov. 2000.

John H. Groberg, "The Power of Keeping the Sabbath Day Holy," *Ensign*, Nov. 1984.

James E. Faust, "The Lord's Day," *Ensign*, Nov. 1991.

Earl C. Tingey, "Keeping the Sabbath Day Holy," *Ensign*, Feb. 2000.

Charles Didier, "The Sabbath—Holy Day or Holiday?" *Ensign*, Oct. 1994.

CHALLENGE

Write a list of all the good things you can do on the Sabbath day. A fantastic resource is the book *Sabbath Solutions* by Trina Boice. It's often listed for free for Amazon Kindle.

DOCTRINAL MASTERY PASSAGES

Book of Mormon
1 Nephi 3:7
Alma 37:35

Old Testament
Exodus 20:3–17
Joshua 24:15

New Testament
John 7:17

John 14:15
Ephesians 4:11–14

Doctrine and Covenants
D&C 14:7
D&C 82:10
D&C 59:9–10

PREACH MY GOSPEL

Pages 22, 25, 71, 72, 74, 76

NOTES

_____

_____

_____

_____

_____

_____

_____

_____

_____

_____

_____

_____

_____

_____

_____

_____

_____

Lesson 15

TRUE DISCIPLES OF
JESUS CHRIST

MUSIC

"I Know That My Redeemer Lives," *Hymns*, no. 136
"Jesus, Lover of My Soul," *Hymns*, no. 102
"I'm Trying to Be like Jesus," *Children's Songbook*, 78
"The Lord Is My Light," *Hymns*, no. 89
"Jesus, the Very Thought of Thee," *Hymns*, no. 141
"Come unto Jesus," *Hymns*, no. 117
"A Poor Wayfaring Man of Grief," *Hymns*, no. 29

SUMMARY

During the October 2018 general conference, Elder Dieter F. Uchtdorf challenged us to become true disciples of Jesus Christ. He declared, "We achieve the abundant life by becoming true disciples of Jesus Christ—by following in His ways and engaging in His work" ("Believe, Love, Do," *Ensign*, Nov. 2018). He taught us that discipleship begins with three simple words: *Believe, love,* and *do.*

First, we must build faith by studying the gospel of Jesus Christ in more depth. The Church's new Sunday adjustments allow for more time to study together as families at home. The more we truly understand the gospel, the more love we will naturally feel for others. The gospel of Jesus Christ can be summed up in one word: love. The Spirit of the Lord is gentle and kind and influences us to *do* good and *be* good.

We need to be patient with others as they learn and grow, and not look for their faults, just as we would hope they would do for us. When we feel God's love deep inside our souls, we feel a desire to reach outside ourselves and bless others. A true understanding of the gospel of Jesus Christ compels us to love and do. Our increased faith leads us to action.

• •

QUOTES

➤ "As disciples of the Savior, we are not merely striving to know more; rather, we need to consistently do more of what we know is right and become better. We should remember that bearing a heartfelt testimony is only a beginning. We need to bear testimony, we need to mean it, and most importantly we need consistently to live it. We need to both declare and live our testimonies." (David A. Bednar, "More Diligent and Concerned at Home," *Ensign*, Nov. 2009, 19.)

➤ "I bear witness that obedience to the gospel plan is the only way to build a Christ-centered life." (Merrill J. Bateman, "Living a Christ-Centered Life," *Ensign*, Jan. 1999.)

➤ "In this, the dispensation of the fulness of time, as we prepare for the final satanic battles in anticipation of the return of Christ to the earth, it is very important to know who is on the Lord's side. The Lord needs to know on whom He can rely." (Robert C. Oaks, "Who's on the Lord's Side? Who?" *Ensign*, Apr. 2005.)

➤ "The Lord has left no doubt in defining His side and where the Saints should be in their thoughts, words, actions, and practices. We have His counsel in the scriptures and in the words of the prophets." (Joseph B. Wirthlin, "The Lord's Side," *Ensign*, Mar. 1993.)

➤ "To follow Christ is to become like Him. It is to learn from His character. As spirit children of our Heavenly Father, we do have the potential to incorporate Christlike attributes into our life and character." (Dieter F. Uchtdorf, "Developing Christlike Attributes," *Ensign*, Oct. 2008.)

• •

GOSPEL ART

Jesus Christ, 1
City of Zion Is Taken Up, 6
Building the Ark, 7
Isaiah Writes of Christ's Birth, 22
Daniel Refusing the King's Meat and Wine, 23

• •

VIDEOS

"What Is Discipleship?": https://www.lds.org/media-library/video/2012-01
-8620-what-is-discipleship

"Discipleship: Three Sisters": https://www.lds.org/media-library/video/topics
/discipleship

"Reflections on a Consecrated Life": http://www.lds.org/media-library/video
/general-conference-october-2010?lang=eng&start=13&end=24#2010
-10-1060-elder-d-todd-christofferson

"Choose This Day": https://www.lds.org/pages/mormon-messages?lang=eng
#choose-this-day

"The Cost—and Blessings—of Discipleship": https://www.lds.org/general
-conference/2014/04/the-cost-and-blessings-of-discipleship

OBJECT LESSONS

- Present three different kinds of chocolate bars to the class, and ask what they have in common (chocolate, sweet, goodness). Cut open a solid chocolate bar, and point out that it represents that God is pure goodness all the way through. Next, cut open a candy bar that has some other things inside. Compare that to a true disciple who is striving to be like God (solid chocolate) but has some imperfections that we all struggle with. Finally, cut open a hollow chocolate egg or bar. Explain that it represents someone who might go to church and appear to be religious, but there is no pure discipleship going on inside.

- Get a large cookie sheet, a large rock to put on the cookie sheet, two cups filled with moist sand, and a large glass of water. Flip one of the cups of sand onto the cookie sheet to make a sand castle. Flip the other cup onto the rock to make another sand castle. Next, pour the water onto the cookie sheet to demonstrate which "house" will survive. The object lesson demonstrates the song "The Wise Man and the Foolish Man." The rock, in this case, represents the gospel of Jesus Christ. Talk about the things a true disciple would use to build his strong house of faith.

ARTICLES

Richard J. Maynes, "Establishing a Christ-Centered Home," *Ensign*, May 2011.

Lawrence E. Corbridge, "Valiant in the Testimony of Jesus Christ," *Ensign*, Sept. 2011.

Clate W. Mask Jr., "Standing Spotless before the Lord," *Ensign*, May 2004.

Stephen A. West, "Are You on the Lord's Side?" *New Era*, Sept. 2002.

Bernard P. Brockbank, "Knowing God," *Ensign*, July 1972, 121–23.

N. Eldon Tanner, "A Basis for Faith in the Living God," *Ensign*, Nov. 1978, 46–49.

L. Tom Perry, "A Pattern for Living," *Liahona*, Jan. 2004.

Howard W. Hunter, "Am I a 'Living' Member?" *Ensign,* May 1987.

CHALLENGE

Look at the list of Christlike qualities that are included on page 115 of *Preach My Gospel*. Evaluate how you are doing in developing those characteristics. Create a plan of action for how you will make Christ more central in your daily thoughts and actions. What changes can you make to focus more on the Savior? What experiences can strengthen your testimony? What goals could you set to become more Christlike in your thoughts, words, and actions?

DOCTRINAL MASTERY PASSAGES

Book of Mormon
1 Nephi 19:23
2 Nephi 32:3
Jacob 2:18–19
Helaman 5:12
3 Nephi 27:27
Moroni 7:16–17
Moroni 10:4–5

Old Testament
Exodus 20:3–17
Deuteronomy 7:3–4
Joshua 24:15
Job 19:25–26
Proverbs 3:5–6
Isaiah 53:3–5
Isaiah 55:8–9

Daniel 2:44–45

New Testament
Matthew 6:24
Luke 24:36–39
John 14:15
John 17:3
Ephesians 4:11–14
Revelation 20:12–13

Doctrine and Covenants
D&C 14:7
D&C 76:22–24
D&C 137:7–10

Joseph Smith—History
JS—H 1:15–20

PREACH MY GOSPEL

Pages 1, 5, 33, 37, 46, 48, 51–54, 60–61, 90, 105, 108, 115–116, 123–126, 198–199

• •

NOTES

_____

_____

_____

_____

_____

_____

_____

_____

_____

_____

_____

_____

_____

_____

_____

_____

Lesson 16

HELPING GOD'S CHILDREN

. . . .

MUSIC

"A Poor Wayfaring Man of Grief," *Hymns*, no. 29
"As Sisters in Zion," *Hymns*, no. 309
"Because I Have Been Given Much," *Hymns*, no. 219
"Have I Done Any Good?" *Hymns*, no. 223
"Let Us Oft Speak Kind Words," *Hymns*, no. 232
"Love One Another," *Hymns*, no. 308

. . . .

SUMMARY

Serving our fellow man, as well as our ward family, has been a consistent theme during general conference during this past decade of unprecedented natural disasters. Sister Cristina B. Franco shared a talk entitled "The Joy of Unselfish Service" at the October 2018 general conference. She reminded us, "We have promised our Father in Heaven that we will serve Him and others with love and do His will in all things" (*Ensign*, Nov. 2018). A true understanding of the gospel of Jesus Christ compels us to love and serve.

If we want to be like Christ, we need to do as Christ did: serve. The Savior ministered daily to the needs of those around Him. When we open our spiritual eyes, we will see many opportunities around us for Christlike service and love. Loving and serving our neighbors isn't always easy, but that great feeling we get afterward is evidence that we're doing exactly what the Savior would do!

Charity is the pure love of Christ and the greatest of all virtues. Charity cannot be developed in the abstract; it requires clinical, hands-on experience.

It is a process, not an event. The more we serve others, the more genuine our love for others will become.

Introduce the class members to several great websites where they can go with their families to choose service projects in their area and reach out to others in their community:

- www.justserve.org
- www.volunteermatch.org
- www.idealist.org
- www.serve.gov
- www.nationalservice.gov

QUOTES

- "The more we serve our fellowmen in appropriate ways, the more substance there is to our souls." (Spencer W. Kimball, "President Kimball Speaks Out on Service to Others," *New Era*, Mar. 1981, 47–49.)
- "We learn that charity, though often quantified as the action, is actually the state of the heart that prompts us to love one another." (Elaine Jack, "Strengthened in Charity," *Ensign*, Nov. 1996.)
- "I am convinced that true brotherly love is essential to our happiness and to world peace. . . . We need to show our love, beginning in the home and then widening our circle of love to encompass our ward members, our less active and nonmember neighbors, and also those who have passed beyond the veil." (Jack H. Goaslind Jr., "Reach Out to Our Father's Children," *Ensign*, May 1981.)
- "Charity is not just a precept or a principle, nor is it just a word to describe actions or attitudes. Rather, it is an internal condition that must be developed and experienced in order to be understood." (C. Max Caldwell, "Love of Christ," *Ensign*, Nov. 1992, 29–30.)
- "When you get the Spirit of God, you feel full of kindness, charity, long-suffering, and you are willing all the day long to accord to every man that which you want yourself." (John Taylor, "Chapter 3: 'Love Thy Neighbour as Thyself,'" *Teachings of Presidents of the Church: John Taylor*, 2011, 20–29.)

GOSPEL ART

The Sermon on the Mount, 39
Christ Healing the Sick at Bethesda, 42

The Good Samaritan, 44
Jesus Washing the Apostles' Feet, 55
Jesus Carrying a Lost Lamb, 64
King Benjamin Addresses His People, 74
Jesus Healing the Nephites, 83
Jesus Blesses the Nephite Children, 84
The Foundation of the Relief Society, 98
Service, 115
Young Couple Going to the Temple, 120

VIDEOS

"JustServe—BYU TV Documentary": https://www.lds.org/media-library/video/topics/service

"Being a More Christian Christian": https://www.lds.org/media-library/video/2012-10-5010-elder-robert-d-hales

"Opportunities to Do Good": https://www.lds.org/media-library/video/2011-10-017-opportunities-to-do-good?category=youth-curriculum/07-july

"Love One Another": http://www.lds.org/ldsorg/v/index.jsp?autoplay=true&index=2&locale=0&sourceId=45a82c0fabfa6210VgnVCM100000176f620a____&vgnextoid=bd163ca6e9aa3210VgnVCM1000003a94610aRCRD

"Love Thy Neighbor": http://www.youtube.com/watch?v=lq5IzDW4ufA

"We Believe in Doing Good to All Men: Service": http://www.youtube.com/watch?v=VXdTNEri1GE&feature=youtube_gdata

"The Good Samaritan": http://lds.org/media-library/video/feature-films?lang=eng#1998-05-01-the-good-samaritan

"Ye Have Done It unto Me": https://www.lds.org/media-library/video/2011-10-068-ye-have-done-it-unto-me

"How Do I Love Thee?—Elder Jeffrey R. Holland" www.lds.org/ldsorg/v/index.jsp?vgnextoid=bd163ca6e9aa3210VgnVCM1000003a94610aRCRD&locale=0

OBJECT LESSONS

→ Sometimes we judge people to determine if they are "worthy" of our acts of service. Carefully peel off a label from a can of mandarin oranges and place it over a can of peas. Present the prepared can to the class along with a regular can of mushrooms, and ask which one you should use in a fruit salad. Of course, the class will want the mandarin oranges. Ask a volunteer to open the can and show it to the group. They should be shocked to see green peas inside. Talk about how we judge people and determine what is best for them. Only Heavenly Father knows what is truly happening in the hearts and lives of His children. He has simply asked us to love and serve.

↦ Write the name of the Church on a large poster and tape it to a sheet. Invite two volunteers to hold the sheet up by both ends. Invite two more volunteers to stand behind the sheet with their heads showing. Next, pass out socks that are folded into little balls to the rest of the class. Invite a few more volunteers to stand between the sheet and the class and challenge them to catch the sock balls that are being thrown by the class. What does all of this demonstrate? There are many people in the world who are experiencing terrible famine, natural disasters, poverty, and violence (the two people behind the sheet), and the Church offers both temporal and spiritual assistance all over the world (the sheet). As members of the Church, we can love and serve all of God's children to ease their burdens. If they join the Church, that's great! If they don't, we have still kept our promise to the Lord by caring for our fellow man.

↦ Teach the members of the class how to knit or crochet so that during your lesson they can begin making leper bandages to send to the Church's Humanitarian Center! You'll find tons of things the members can do to serve at www.ldsphilanthropies.org.

Items can be sent to

> LDS Philanthropies
> 15 E. South Temple
> 2nd Floor East
> Salt Lake City, UT 84150
> Telephone: (801) 240-5567

• •

ARTICLES

V. Dallas Merrell, "A Vision of Service," *Ensign*, Dec. 1996, 10–15.

C. Max Caldwell, "Love of Christ," *Ensign*, Nov. 1992, 29–30.

Gene R. Cook, "Charity: Perfect and Everlasting Love," *Ensign*, May 2002, 82–83.

Bonnie D. Parkin, "Choosing Charity: That Good Part," *Ensign*, Nov. 2003, 104–106.

Henry B. Eyring, "Feeding His Lambs," *Liahona*, Feb. 2008.

Derek A. Cuthbert, "The Spirituality of Service," *Ensign*, May 1990, 12–13.
Jeffrey R. Holland, "Charity Never Faileth," *Liahona*, Mar. 2011.
Spencer W. Kimball, "Small Acts of Service," *Ensign*, Dec. 1974, 2–7.
Russell C. Taylor, "The Joy of Service," *Ensign*, Nov. 1984, 23–24.
Gene R. Cook, "Charity: Perfect and Everlasting Love," *Ensign*, May 2002, 82–83.

• •

CHALLENGE

Talk to your Relief Society president, compassionate service leader, or elders quorum president to see what you can do to serve. Who needs help in your ward? What non-members in your area are struggling? How could you help them? Your service can be anonymous or done in the name of the Church. Find out if the Church's "Helping Hands" program needs volunteers in your area. You can learn more about their community service and disaster relief projects at https://www.lds.org/topics/humanitarian-service/helping-hands?lang=eng&old=true. You can also find local service projects at www.justserve.org.

• •

DOCTRINAL MASTERY PASSAGES

Book of Mormon
2 Nephi 28:7–9
Jacob 2:18–19
Mosiah 2:17
3 Nephi 11:29
Moroni 7:45

Old Testament
Leviticus 19:18

Doctrine and Covenants
D&C 64:9–11
D&C 88:123–24

Pearl of Great Price
Moses 7:18

• •

PREACH MY GOSPEL

Pages 2, 8, 62, 87, 115, 118, 123–126, 168–169

• •

NOTES

Lesson 17

THE BOOK OF MORMON

MUSIC

"As I Search the Holy Scriptures," *Hymns*, no. 277
"Book of Mormon Stories," *Children's Songbook*, 118
"From Homes of Saints Glad Songs Arise," *Hymns*, no. 297
"The Books in the Book of Mormon," *Children's Songbook*, 119
"Search, Ponder, and Pray," *Children's Songbook*, 109

SUMMARY

Elder Shayne M. Bowen of the Seventy talked about the role of the Book of Mormon in conversion during the October 2018 general conference. He explained, "We are gathering Israel for the last time and are doing so with the Book of Mormon—a book that, combined with the Spirit of the Lord, is the most powerful tool of conversion" ("The Role of the Book of Mormon in Conversion," *Ensign*, Nov. 2018).

We can find more comfort and wisdom in the Book of Mormon than in all other books ever written. The Book of Mormon is a sacred record that contains the fulness of the gospel and testifies that Jesus Christ is the Redeemer of the world.

The Law of Witnesses was fulfilled by three men who gave testimony when they saw an angel and the gold plates while hearing God's voice, as well as eight other men who handled the plates with their own hands. Each setting was different, but both experiences never left doubt in the minds and hearts of the witnesses for the rest of their lives. Each of us can be a witness of the Book of Mormon too.

• •

QUOTES

➥ "Each of us, at some time in our lives, must discover the scriptures for ourselves—and not just discover them once, but rediscover them again and again." (Spencer W. Kimball, "How Rare a Possession—the Scriptures!" *Tambuli,* Dec. 1985, 2–5; or *Ensign,* Sept. 1976, 2–5.)

➥ "I told the brethren that the Book of Mormon was the most correct of any book on earth, and the keystone of our religion, and a man would get nearer to God by abiding by its precepts than by any other book." (Joseph Smith Jr., *History of The Church of Jesus Christ of Latter-day Saints,* 4:461.)

➥ "I knew it was true, as well as I knew that I could see with my eyes, or feel by the touch of my fingers, or be sensible of the demonstration of any sense." (Brigham Young, *Journal of Discourses,* 3:91.)

➥ "The Book of Mormon is truly a witness for Jesus Christ and his plan of salvation for mankind. It is a witness that Jesus Christ, through Joseph Smith, has again established his work in our day. We invite all mankind to read it and learn for themselves its powerful message." (James A. Cullimore, "The Book of Mormon," *Ensign,* May 1976.)

• •

GOSPEL ART

Moroni Hides the Plates in the Hill Cumorah, 86
Joseph Smith Seeks Wisdom in the Bible, 89

• •

VIDEOS

"President Eyring on the Book of Mormon": https://www.lds.org/media -library/video/2011-10-64-president-eyring-on-the-book-of-mormon ?category=topics/book-of-mormon

"A Book with a Promise": https://www.lds.org/pages/mormon-messages

"Prepared for Our Day": https://www.lds.org/media-library/video/2012-08 -3110-prepared-for-our-day

"Book of Mormon Testimonies": https://www.lds.org/media-library/video /2011-06-8-book-of-mormon-testimonies

"Another Testament of Jesus Christ—Richard": http://lds.org/media-library /video/truth-restored

"What Is the Role of the Book of Mormon?": https://www.lds.org/manual/preach-my-gospel/asl/chapter5

OBJECT LESSONS

☞ With a white crayon, write the words "The Book of Mormon" on a white piece of paper. Show the other side of the white paper to the class so they can't see the crayon marks, and explain that Jesus talked about His "other sheep" who would hear His gospel (3 Nephi 15:17). Loosely roll the white paper so that it fits inside a clear glass that has water with red food coloring in it. Talk about Christ's death and Resurrection. (The red water represents the blood that was shed for us.) Carefully remove the white paper, and the writing should now appear. It wasn't until hundreds of years after Christ's death that the Book of Mormon emerged and we were able to learn who those "other sheep" were!

☞ Take apart a flashlight, and give several volunteers one piece each to hold up in front of the class. Ask them if they can make light from their one piece. (No.) Invite another volunteer to carefully gather all of the pieces and build the flashlight. Now the light can turn on for everyone! Explain that before the Restoration, there were pieces of truth, but they were separated. The Restoration of the gospel and discovery of the Book of Mormon brought these pieces together and gave light to a very dark world!

☞ Show the class an old, rotten banana and ask for a volunteer to eat it. (No one will want to.) Ask the class why they don't think it will taste very good. Now hold up a good banana and ask why anyone would choose to eat this one. Explain that our lives are like fruit; people can tell what kind of people we are by the fruit we produce. Matthew 7:20 says, 'Wherefore by their fruits ye shall know them." Ask, "What kind of fruit do you want to produce?" The Book of Mormon is the fruit that evidences the truthfulness of Joseph Smith's testimony. You may be the only Book of Mormon people will ever "read." Live your lives so that others can tell you're a disciple of Christ and will want to know more.

ARTICLES

Shayne M. Bowen, "The Role of the Book of Mormon in Conversion," *Ensign*, Nov. 2018.
Thomas S. Monson, "The Power of the Book of Mormon," *Ensign*, May 2017.

Tad R. Callister, "God's Compelling Witness: The Book of Mormon," *Ensign*, Nov. 2017.

Ezra Taft Benson, "The Book of Mormon Is the Word of God," *Ensign*, Jan. 1988.

Daniel C. Peterson, "Mounting Evidence for the Book of Mormon," *Ensign*, Jan. 2000.

L. Tom Perry, "'Give Heed unto the Word of the Lord,'" *Ensign*, June 2000.

• •

CHALLENGE

Set a goal to read the Book of Mormon this year in your personal scripture study. Calculate how many pages a day you'll need to read to accomplish your objective. A really quick and easy resource is the Book of Mormon calculator website at http://www.bookofmormoncalculator.com.

• •

DOCTRINAL MASTERY PASSAGES

Book of Mormon
Alma 37:6–7
Moroni 10:4–5

Old Testament
Isaiah 29:13–14
Ezekiel 37:15–17

New Testament
John 10:16
2 Thessalonians 2:1–3
2 Timothy 3:16–17
James 1:5–6
Revelation 14:6–7

• •

PREACH MY GOSPEL

Pages 7, 38–39, 103–4, 110–111, 103–114, 130

• •

NOTES

_____

_____

_____

_____

Lesson 18

SEEKING OUT THE
LOST SHEEP

MUSIC

"Dear to the Heart of the Shepherd," *Hymns*, no. 221
"The Lord Is My Shepherd," *Hymns*, no. 108
"Come, All Whose Souls Are Lighted," *Hymns*, no. 268
"Come, All Ye Saints of Zion," *Hymns*, no. 38

SUMMARY

Elder Gary E. Stevenson spoke in the October 2018 general conference about shepherding souls. He reminded us, "We reach out in love to others because it is what our Savior commanded us to do" ("Shepherding Souls," *Ensign*, Nov. 2018).

The parable of the lost sheep teaches us about the love of the Savior for the one. It is a sacred duty and honor to help the Lord feed His sheep and find those who are lost. With kindness and patience, we can befriend those who are less active in the Church and help them feel the joy and influence of the Spirit.

With the companionship of the Holy Ghost, we can receive inspiration about what to say and how to invite less-active members back into the fold. The goal is to help them remember the sacred covenants they made at baptism and to gain a desire to participate in additional ordinances that will bless their lives.

Being a good shepherd also means to fellowship the newly baptized converts in our ward family. Keep in touch with the ward missionaries and ward mission leader to find out when the next baptism will be and how you can offer a friendly hand before and after the exciting event. Plan to sit next to new converts in sacrament meeting, or invite them to join you for family home evening. Joining the Church can be scary and lonely. Your shepherding efforts can help new and returning members feel like a part of the flock quickly.

Elder Ulisses Soares gave a talk in the October 2018 general conference that inspired us to reach out to non-members and new members of the Church. He explained, "Those of us who are at different points in the long journey of discipleship must extend a warm hand of fellowship to our new friends, accept them where they are, and help, love, and include them in our lives" ("One in Christ," *Ensign*, Nov. 2018).

QUOTES

- "It is not good to make others feel as though they are deficient. Let us lift those around us. Let us extend a welcoming hand. Let us bestow upon our brothers and sisters a special measure of humanity, compassion, and charity so that they feel, at long last, they have finally found home." (Dieter F. Uchtdorf, "'You Are My Hands,'" *Ensign*, May 2010.)

- "Jesus said, 'Feed my sheep' (John 21:16). You can't feed them if you don't know where they are. You can't feed them if you give them reason to resist you. The best foods with which to feed His sheep are charity and the restoration of dignity. By our actions we show our love." (Marvin J. Ashton, in Conference Report, *Ensign*, Oct. 1981, 128–129.)

- "So often what people need so much is to be sheltered from the storms of life in the sanctuary of belonging." (Neal A. Maxwell, *The Neal A. Maxwell Quote Book*, 1997, 125.)

- "Whenever I think of the shepherd's loving and caring efforts on behalf of the one, I'm reminded of the Savior's deep and abiding love for each of us. Oh, how He rejoices when a lost soul is found by a faithful undershepherd and then is tenderly and lovingly brought home again!" (Alexander B. Morrison, "Nourish the Flock of Christ," *Ensign*, May 1992.)

- "Conversion requires consecrating our lives to caring for and serving others who need our help and to sharing our gifts and talents. The Lord didn't say tend my sheep when it is convenient, watch my sheep when you aren't busy. He said feed my sheep and my lambs; help them survive this world, keep them close to you. Lead them to safety—the safety of righteous choices that will prepare them for eternal life." (Robert D. Hales, "'When Thou Art Converted, Strengthen Thy Brethren,'" *Ensign*, May 1997.)

GOSPEL ART

The Sermon on the Mount, 39
The Good Samaritan, 44
Go Ye Therefore, 61
Jesus Carrying a Lost Lamb, 64
Jesus at the Door, 65
The Foundation of the Relief Society, 98
Service, 115

VIDEOS

"Fellowshipping 1": https://www.lds.org/media-library/video/2012-08-3230
-fellowshipping-1
"Fellowshipping 2": https://www.lds.org/media-library/video/2012-08-3235
-fellowshipping-2
"Feed My Sheep": https://www.lds.org/media-library/video/2014-01-025-feed
-my-sheep
"Jesus Declares the Parable of the Lost Sheep": https://www.lds.org/media
-library/video/2011-10-063-jesus-declares-the-parable-of-the-lost-sheep
"Ye Have Done It unto Me": https://www.lds.org/media-library/video/2011
-10-068-ye-have-done-it-unto-me
"The Good Shepherd": https://www.lds.org/media-library/video/2013-10-1550
-the-good-shepherd
"Waiting for the Prodigal": https://www.lds.org/media-library/video/2015
-04-4050-elder-brent-h-nielson

OBJECT LESSONS

- Lock all of the doors to the classroom so that there is only one entrance. At
the entrance, place one of those Cub Scout/Boy Scout crossover bridges, if
you can find one. Have a volunteer stand at the bridge to help people over
it as they sit down. During the lesson, talk about what that bridge might
represent in our lives (baptism into the Church) as well as the person helping them over it (ministering member). Discuss why someone might want
to go back over the bridge to leave and what difference it might make

if there were more volunteers helping the class members cross over the bridge to find a comfortable chair to sit in.

- Have the class listen to the voices of Apostles and prophets and try to guess whose voices they are. Then play some voices of members of their family. Talk about how it is much easier to recognize a voice when you are familiar with it. We need to develop relationships of trust with our less-active friends so that they can feel comfortable and safe returning to the Church. Talk about ways we can get to know new members and less active members to help them with their challenges.

- Play "four corners" so the class can get to know each other better. Then follow up with explaining how it's easier to serve others when we know a little bit about them and what we might have in common. How to play the game: Tell the class a series of lists of four things to choose from, and assign a corner of the room to each one. Invite them to stand in the corner that best represents their answer. Questions might include things like "What is your favorite season of the year?" (winter, spring, summer, or fall); "Who is your favorite scripture hero?" (Moses, Paul, Nephi, or Captain Moroni); "What is your favorite dessert?" (cheesecake, ice cream, anything chocolate, or pie); "Where is your favorite place to go on vacation?" (beach, mountains, big city, or staycation); and "Which temple is your favorite?" (Salt Lake City, San Diego, the one closest to your home, or Nauvoo).

ARTICLES

Ned B. Roueché, "Fellowshipping," *Ensign*, May 1999.
Gérald Caussé, "Ye Are No More Strangers," *Ensign*, Nov. 2013.
Mervyn B. Arnold, "To the Rescue: We Can Do It," *Ensign*, May 2016.
Silvia H. Allred, "Feed My Sheep," *Ensign*, Nov. 2007.
Ulisses Soares, "'Feed My Sheep,'" *Ensign*, Nov. 2005.
James E. Faust, "Dear Are the Sheep That Have Wandered," *Ensign*, June 2013.
Gordon B. Hinckley, "Find the Lambs, Feed the Sheep," *Ensign*, May 1999.
Joseph B. Wirthlin, "Restoring the Lost Sheep," *Ensign*, May 1984.
Robert D. Hales, "When Thou Art Converted, Strengthen Thy Brethren," *Ensign*, May 1997.

CHALLENGE

Look at your list of the people you are assigned to minister to. What do you have in common with them? If you don't know, find out! Write a list of activities inside and outside of church that you could invite them to. Find someone who knows them well to get ideas of things they like. "Friend" them on social media, and start sending them uplifting messages to develop a friendship.

• •

DOCTRINAL MASTERY PASSAGES

Book of Mormon
2 Nephi 32:3
Moroni 10:4–5

Doctrine and Covenants
D&C 8:2–3
D&C 130:22–23

New Testament
James 1:5–6

• •

PREACH MY GOSPEL

Pages 3, 18, 65, 89–93, 96–102

• •

NOTES

_____

_____

_____

_____

_____

_____

_____

_____

_____

_____

Lesson 19

THE GATHERING OF ISRAEL THROUGH OUR MISSIONARY EFFORTS

· ·

MUSIC

"Called to Serve," *Hymns*, no. 249
"How Will They Know?" *Children's Songbook*, 182
"I Hope They Call Me on a Mission," *Children's Songbook*, 169
"I Want to Be a Missionary Now," *Children's Songbook*, 168
"We'll Bring the World His Truth," *Children's Songbook*, 172

· ·

SUMMARY

The Church released a letter on October 6, 2018, announcing new policies regarding the Relief Society and the elders quorum and their responsibilities toward missionary work. Each presidency is to assign a counselor who will help coordinate missionary efforts in the ward. The members of the ward should support missionary work in their quorums and Relief Society classes, working together as a team.

There are many people in the world who are pure in heart, who would embrace the fulness of the gospel if they were given the opportunity. We have been given the knowledge of saving ordinances as well as the divinely commissioned authority to provide them to the nations of the earth.

When we truly feel the Savior's love, we have the natural desire to extend it to those around us. When we do, our joy will be felt for eternity. The Lord entrusts us with this important work, and it is our privilege to bring light to a dark world. Our righteous examples can illuminate our neighborhoods and draw the pure in heart to us.

In the spirit of love and kindness, our missionary work is about inviting people, not convincing them, to learn more. Rather than debate doctrine with non-believers, we show them the Savior's love. The most important part of effective missionary work is not our carefully chosen words but the Spirit with which we teach. This is the Lord's work and one of the most important things we can do here on earth.

When we help prepare young men and women to serve full-time missions and support them with prayers, food, finances, and referrals while they are laboring in the field, the Lord is pleased with our missionary efforts, and we will have an even greater desire to open our mouths and share what we know with a world that is seeking truth and direction. What a thrill it is to be a part of the exciting wave of missionary work happening right now as the Lord hastens His work!

Older couples should also begin preparing to serve full-time missions. With the combined efforts of full-time missionaries and ward members, the Church can gather Israel for the Lord's Second Coming.

* *

QUOTES

- "If we were fully united as a people in our missionary work, we would rapidly hasten the day when the gospel would be preached to all people without and within the boundaries of the organized stakes of Zion." (Harold B. Lee, "Strengthen the Stakes of Zion," in Conference Report, Apr. 1950.)

- "As members of the Lord's Church, we must take missionary work more seriously. The Lord's commission to 'preach the gospel to every creature' (Mark 16:15) will never change in our dispensation. We have been greatly blessed with the material means, the technology, and an inspired message to bring the gospel to all men. More is expected of us than any previous generation." (Ezra Taft Benson, "Our Responsibility to Share the Gospel," *Ensign*, May 1985.)

- "This isn't missionary work. This is missionary fun." (Neil L. Anderson, "It's a Miracle," *Ensign*, May 2013.)

- "We must develop love for people. Our hearts must go out to them in the pure love of the gospel, in a desire to lift them, to build them up, to point them to a higher, finer life that eventually will lead to exaltation in the celestial kingdom of God." (Ezra Taft Benson, "Keys to Successful Member-Missionary Work," *Ensign*, Sept. 1990.)

⊷ "For the Savior's mandate to share the gospel to become part of who we are, we need to make member missionary work a way of life." (Quentin L. Cook, "Be a Missionary All Your Life," *Ensign*, Sept. 2008.)

⊷ "It is impractical for us to expect that full-time missionaries alone can warn the millions in the world. Members must be finders. If we are in tune, the Spirit of the Lord will speak to us and guide us to those with whom we should share the gospel. The Lord will help us if we will but listen." (Spencer W. Kimball, as quoted by Ezra Taft Benson, "President Kimball's Vision of Missionary Work," *Ensign*, July 1985.)

⊷ "When we received the special blessing of knowledge of the gospel of Jesus Christ and took upon ourselves the name of Christ by entering the waters of baptism, we also accepted the obligation to share the gospel with others." (L. Tom Perry, "The Past Way of Facing the Future," *Ensign*, Nov. 2009, 75.)

⊷ "After all that has been said, the greatest and most important duty is to preach the Gospel." (Joseph Smith, *History of The Church of Jesus Christ of Latter-day Saints*, 2:478.)

• •

GOSPEL ART

Esther, 21
Boy Jesus in the Temple, 34
Calling of the Fishermen, 37
Go Ye Therefore, 61
Abinadi before King Noah, 75
Alma Baptizes in the Waters of Mormon, 76
Ammon Defends the Flocks of King Lamoni, 78
Missionaries: Elders, 109
Missionaries: Sisters, 110

• •

VIDEOS

"Hasten the Work" is a new video series with many videos about missionary work! You can see them all at https://www.lds.org/media-library/video /categories/hasten-the-work.

"Missionary Work": https://www.lds.org/manual/preach-my-gospel/asl/chap
ter3/lesson5?lang=eng#missionary-work

"The Church to Fill the Earth": https://www.lds.org/media-library/video
/2010-07-059-the-church-to-fill-the-earth

"Developing the Faith to Find": https://www.lds.org/media-library/video
/2007-04-024-developing-the-faith-to-find

"Why Mormons Send Missionaries around the World": https://www.lds.org
/media-library/video/2010-05-1190-why-mormons-send-missionaries
-around-the-world

"Ward Councils and Ward Mission Leaders": https://www.lds.org/media
-library/video/hasten-the-work/ward-councils-and-ward-mission-leaders

• •

OBJECT LESSONS

r–• Show your class a few raw eggs and one hard-boiled egg, and ask if they
can tell which one is the hard-boiled egg. They should all be white and
look the same. If someone is very confident, ask him or her if he or she
is sure enough to have you crack it over his or her head. (He or she will
probably be less confident with their guess!) Only the Lord knows which
people are ready to accept the gospel and which ones are not. Are there
signs to help us? Spin the eggs on a table. The one that is hard-boiled
should spin longer on its side. Crack the eggs into a bowl to see who
guessed correctly which egg was hard-boiled. The truth is that we have
been commanded to share the gospel with the whole world!

r–• Set up a row of dominoes on the front table, and then watch the chain
reaction as you knock the first one down. Compare that to all of the lives
that are touched for good by just one member of the Church being a good
missionary.

r–• Display a large basket of goodies on the table at the front of the class and
begin to eat from it, expressing great delight. Ask the class to share why they
love the gospel so much. Continue snacking, and then explain that when
we enjoy the blessings of the gospel without sharing it with others, it's like
having a basket of goodies that you love and not sharing it with the class!
Pass the basket around, and invite everyone to join you in eating yummy
treats. At the end of the lesson, ask the class how many of them didn't take
a treat, how many ate it right away, and how many planned on saving it
for later. Explain that doing missionary work is similar—even when we
share the sweet gospel with others, some people will accept and embrace it,
others won't at all, and others might eventually after many years.

• •

ARTICLES

David A. Bednar, "Called to the Work" *Ensign*, May 2017.
S. Gifford Nielsen, "Hastening the Lord's Game Plan!" *Ensign*, Nov. 2013.
Earl C. Tingey, "Missionary Service," *Ensign*, May 1998, 39–41.
Thomas S. Monson, "That All May Hear," *Ensign*, May 1995.
M. Russell Ballard, "Creating a Gospel-Sharing Home," *Ensign*, May 2006.
Dallin H. Oaks, "Sharing the Restored Gospel," *Ensign*, Nov. 2016.
Dallin H. Oaks, "The Role of Members in Conversion," *Ensign*, Mar. 2003, 52.
Ezra Taft Benson, "President Kimball's Vision of Missionary Work," *Ensign*, July 1985.

• •

CHALLENGE

Invite the full-time missionaries in your area over to dinner. Ask them about their investigators, and find out what you can do to help. Invite them to teach one of their investigators in your home, or volunteer to go with them to teach.

• •

DOCTRINAL MASTERY PASSAGES

Book of Mormon
Moroni 10:4–5

Old Testament
Isaiah 29:13–14
Jeremiah 16:16

New Testament
Romans 1:16

Revelation 14:6–7

Doctrine and Covenants
D&C 18:10, 15–16

Joseph Smith—History
JS—H 1:15–20

• •

PREACH MY GOSPEL

Pages 1, 2, 4–5, 8–13, 19, 20–21, 44–45, 81, 105, 107, 108, 127, 138, 139, 155–158, 174–176, 182–187, 190–192, 195–199, 203

• •

NOTES

Lesson 20

LIFE AFTER DEATH

MUSIC

"I Lived in Heaven," *Children's Songbook*, 4
"My Redeemer Lives," *Hymns*, no. 135
"Upon the Cross of Calvary," *Hymns*, no. 184
"O Thou, Before the World Began," *Hymns*, no. 189
"God Be with You Till We Meet Again," *Hymns*, no. 152

SUMMARY

There is probably no doctrine that is more reassuring and comforting than knowing there is life after death. Elder M. Russell Ballard assured us of this truth at the October 2018 general conference. His dear wife had just passed away when he gave his sweet talk. He shared the story behind the revelation of the redemption of the dead in Doctrine and Covenants 138 and stated, "We too can be comforted and learn more about our own future when we and our loved ones die and go to the spirit world by studying this revelation and pondering its significance in the way we live our lives each day" ("The Vision of the Redemption of the Dead," *Ensign*, Nov. 2018).

Each one of us is a son or daughter of a loving Heavenly Father, who gave us the opportunity to come to earth to learn and grow. We lived before we came here as spirits, and we will continue to live after our bodies die. God created a plan of happiness for us so that we can become like Him. A Grand Council in heaven taught us that we would have agency to choose good or evil on earth and that a Savior would be provided for us to help us overcome both spiritual and physical death.

• •

QUOTES

╺● "All of us have to deal with death at one time or another, but to have in one's heart a solid conviction concerning the reality of eternal life is to bring a sense of peace in an hour of tragedy that can come from no other source under the heavens." (Gordon B. Hinckley, *Teachings of Gordon B. Hinckley*, 1997, 153.)

╺● "It is true. We live to die, and we die to live again. From an eternal perspective, the only death that is truly premature is the death of one who is not prepared to meet God." (Russell M. Nelson, "Face the Future with Faith," *Ensign*, May 2011.)

╺● "The Lord has carefully provided a plan of life called the plan of salvation. It comprises all of the laws, ordinances, principles, and doctrines required to complete our mortal journey and progress to a state of exaltation enjoyed by our Father in Heaven." (Duane B. Gerrard, "The Plan of Salvation: A Flight Plan for Life," *Ensign*, Nov. 1997.)

╺● "Now is the time to prepare. Then, when death comes, we can move toward the celestial glory that Heavenly Father has prepared for His faithful children. Meanwhile, for sorrowing loved ones left behind . . . the sting of death is soothed by a steadfast faith in Christ, a perfect brightness of hope, a love of God and of all men, and a deep desire to them." (Russell M. Nelson, "Now Is the Time to Prepare," *Ensign*, May 2005.)

╺● "We can't fully appreciate joyful reunions later without tearful separations now. The only way to take sorrow out of death is to take love out of life." (Russell M. Nelson, "Doors of Death," *Ensign*, May 1992.)

• •

GOSPEL ART

City of Zion Is Taken Up, 6
Isaiah Writes of Christ's Birth, 22
The Annunciation: The Angel Gabriel Appears to Mary, 28
The Angel Appears to the Shepherds, 31
Jesus Raising Jairus's Daughter, 41
Jesus Raising Lazarus from the Dead, 49
Mary and the Resurrected Jesus Christ, 59
Jesus Shows His Wounds, 60
The Ascension of Jesus, 61
Stephen Sees Jesus on the Right Hand of God, 63

The Second Coming, 66
Jesus Teaching in the Western Hemisphere, 82
The Brother of Jared Sees the Finger of the Lord, 85
The First Vision, 90
Moroni Appears to Joseph Smith in His Room, 91
John the Baptist Conferring the Aaronic Priesthood, 93
Melchizedek Priesthood Restoration, 94
Elijah Appearing in the Kirtland Temple, 95

• •

VIDEOS

"Life after Death—Jean": https://www.lds.org/media-library/video/2009-04
-040-life-after-death-jean
"What Happens after We Die?": https://www.lds.org/media-library/video
/2015-08-1080-what-happens-after-we-die
"Death Is Swallowed Up in Christ": https://www.lds.org/media-library/video
/2013-10-1930-death-is-swallowed-up-in-christ?category=new-testament
/acts-revelation
"Our Heavenly Father's Plan": https://www.lds.org/media-library/video
/missionary/our-heavenly-fathers-plan
"Man's Search for Happiness": https://www.lds.org/media-library/video
/feature-films/2016-10-0002-mans-search-for-happiness-1986

• •

OBJECT LESSONS

- Create an ice sculpture to display on the table at the front of the class. I'm KIDDING!
- Give everyone a small bag of granulated sugar at the beginning of the lesson. Explain that every human being ever born has been given the sweet gift of the Atonement, the opportunity to be resurrected and live again after this life. At the end of the lesson, trade the bag of sugar for a candy bar to show that we can all live again (sweet!) but that our reward can be made even greater if we are obedient and follow the commandments in this life.
- Display a bunch of different kinds of shoes at the front of the class. Talk about how we are all born into different situations in this life. For example, some will be born in the country (cowboy boots), others will be born near the beach (flip-flops), and some will arrive in a home in the jungle

(sandals). Some people may be born into bodies that are extremely athletic (sports shoes) while others are born into riches (high heels). You can give more fun examples to make the point that we have no control over where we begin life. Next, show the class some nail clippers and toe corn pads, explaining that they represent the rough times we might have in life. Display socks, and ask the class what they think they represent. Socks could symbolize the people who have found the warmth of the gospel in this life. Finally, show the class a bottle of foot lotion and ask how that could represent life after death. The lotion soothes our troubled feet from this world and allows them to rest in the next world. Give everyone a small bottle of lotion. You might be able to get a hotel to donate some bottles of lotion to pass out to your class!

→ To taste the differences between the degrees of glory, offer the class bites of chocolate and ask which they'd prefer for eternity:
1. No chocolate = outer darkness
2. Unsweetened chocolate = telestial kingdom
3. Bittersweet chocolate = terrestrial kingdom
4. Milk chocolate = celestial kingdom

ARTICLES

Russell M. Nelson, "Doors of Death," *Ensign*, May 1992.
Russell M. Nelson, "Life after Life," *Ensign*, May 1987.
Carlos E. Asay, "'If a Man Die, Shall He Live Again?'" *Ensign*, May 1994.
LeGrand Richards, "What After Death?" *Ensign*, Nov. 1974.
Ezra Taft Benson, "Life Is Eternal," *Ensign*, June 1971.
Franklin D. Richards, "The Message of Easter," *Ensign*, May 1975.

CHALLENGE

Place flags on the graves of fallen soldiers during a patriotic holiday to honor their service. Flags are to be placed over the area on the ground where their heart would be while lying down.

DOCTRINAL MASTERY PASSAGES

Book of Mormon
Alma 34:32–34

Old Testament
Job 19:25–26

Malachi 4:5–6

New Testament
John 17:3
Acts 7:55–56
1 Corinthians 15:20–22
1 Corinthians 15:29
1 Corinthians 15:40–42
Revelation 20:12–13

Doctrine and Covenants
D&C 1:37–38

D&C 18:10, 15–16
D&C 76:22–24
D&C 130:18–19
D&C 130:20–21
D&C 131:1–4
D&C 137:7–10

Pearl of Great Price
Moses 1:39

PREACH MY GOSPEL

Pages 48, 50, 52, 53 54, 58, 59

NOTES

Lesson 21

CULTURE OF KINDNESS

. . . .

MUSIC

"Because I Have Been Given Much," *Hymns*, no. 219
"Love One Another," *Hymns*, no. 308
"'Tis Sweet to Sing the Matchless Love," *Hymns*, no. 177
"Truth Reflects upon Our Senses," *Hymns*, no. 273
"We Have Partaken of Thy Love," *Hymns*, no. 155

. . . .

SUMMARY

Primary General President Joy D. Jones reminded us during the October 2018 general conference that the reason we are kind and serve others is that we love the Lord. She revealed, "I testify that when Jesus Christ, through the power of His Atonement, works on us and in us, He begins to work through us to bless others" ("For Him," *Ensign*, Nov. 2018). When we are kind or when we serve others, we build a more perfect relationship with our Heavenly Father. We are able to show kindness and love to our neighbors when we truly love God.

When we show kindness inside and outside our home, hearts are softened and peace is given to a troubled world. Sometimes we are the least kind to our family members because we take them for granted. Kindness begins at home. Home is the perfect place to practice showing kindness each day until it becomes a natural habit that extends beyond our four walls.

. . . .

QUOTES

➤ "There is no end to the good we can do, to the influence we can have with others. Let us not dwell on the critical or the negative. Let us pray for strength; let us pray for capacity and desire to assist others. Let us radiate the light of the gospel at all times and all places, that the Spirit of the Redeemer may radiate from us." (Gordon B. Hinckley, "The Need for Greater Kindness," *Ensign*, May 2006.)

➻ "Kindness is the essence of greatness and the fundamental characteristic of the noblest men and women I have known. Kindness is a passport that opens doors and fashions friends. It softens hearts and molds relationships that can last lifetimes." (Joseph B. Wirthlin, "The Virtue of Kindness," *Ensign*, May 2005.)

➻ "Kindness has many synonyms—love, service, charity. But I like the word *kindness* because it implies action. It seems like something you and I can do. Kindness can be shown in so many ways." (Betty Jo Jepsen, "Kindness—A Part of God's Plan," *Ensign*, Nov. 1990.)

➻ "Courtesy, respect, deference, and kind consideration are all pleasing attributes that may be shown on all occasions, and wherever manifested contribute to the pleasure and sweetness of human relations." (David O. McKay, in Conference Report, Oct. 1955.)

GOSPEL ART

Jesus Christ, 1
City of Zion Is Taken Up, 6
The Sermon on the Mount, 39
Christ Healing the Sick at Bethesda, 42
The Good Samaritan, 44
Jesus Washing the Apostles' Feet, 55
Jesus Carrying a Lost Lamb, 64
King Benjamin Addresses His People, 74
Jesus Healing the Nephites, 83
Jesus Blesses the Nephite Children, 84
The Foundation of the Relief Society, 98
Service, 115
Young Couple Going to the Temple, 120

VIDEOS

"The Need for Greater Kindness": https://www.lds.org/media-library/video/2006-04-3060-president-gordon-b-hinckley
"Tayla's Kindness": https://www.lds.org/media-library/video/2012-01-009-talyas-kindness
"Service": https://www.lds.org/media-library/video/topics/service
"Criticism": https://www.lds.org/media-library/video/topics/criticism
"Looking through Windows": https://www.lds.org/media-library/video/2012-01-004-looking-through-windows?category=topics/criticism

OBJECT LESSONS

- Get one of the small travel-sized tubes of toothpaste, and invite a volunteer to squeeze all of the toothpaste out onto a large plate while pretending to complain about the bad weather. Next, invite another volunteer to put all of the toothpaste back into the tube. Give the volunteer tools like toothpicks, a toothbrush, and a straw. Obviously, it's extremely hard to do. Compare the experiment to the words that come out of our mouth. Once we have spoken words, people can't "un-hear" them. This also applies to words we post on social media. When we complain, gossip, or speak unkindly, we can ask for forgiveness, but the hurtful effects can still linger.
- Divide the class into groups, and challenge them to create an object lesson that illustrates the importance of kindness. You will be impressed with how creative they can be!
- Display a Russian nesting doll, and then show the class how it works, by removing each of the dolls and handing each to several volunteers, who stand at the front of the classroom. Talk about how kindness has a ripple effect. Have each volunteer think of a kind word or action. As they say their act of kindness, gather the dolls back together, illustrating that when we treat others with love, we become one.

ARTICLES

Joseph B. Wirthlin, "The Virtue of Kindness," *Liahona*, May 2005.
Betty Jo Jepsen, "Kindness—A Part of God's Plan," *Ensign*, Nov. 1990.
Milly Day, "Kindness, Goodwill, Generosity," *Ensign*, Jan. 1998.
Gordon B. Hinckley, "The Need for Greater Kindness," *Ensign*, May 2006.

Susan Hainsworth, "If You Would Serve Them, Love Them," *Ensign*, Mar. 1986.

Mary N. Cook, "'Remember This: Kindness Begins with Me,'" *Ensign*, May 2011.

C. Max Caldwell, "Love of Christ," *Ensign*, Nov. 1992, 29–30.

• •

CHALLENGE

Do something kind for someone without getting credit. In other words, give anonymous service. It can be something simple like putting a little gift on someone's doorstep, sending flowers, making someone's bed, doing a household chore, writing a letter, etc.

• •

DOCTRINAL MASTERY PASSAGES

Book of Mormon
1 Nephi 3:7
Jacob 2:18–19
Mosiah 2:17
Mosiah 4:30
Moroni 7:45

Old Testament
Leviticus 19:18

New Testament
Matthew 5:14–16
Matthew 25:40

Doctrine and Covenants
D&C 84:33–39
D&C 137:7–10

• •

PREACH MY GOSPEL

Pages 118, 168, 169

• •

NOTES

_____
_____
_____
_____

Lesson 22

FAMILY HISTORY AND TEMPLE SERVICE

MUSIC

"Families Can Be Together Forever," *Hymns*, no. 300
"God Is in His Holy Temple," *Hymns*, no. 132
"High on the Mountain Top," *Hymns*, no. 5
"Holy Temples on Mount Zion," *Hymns*, no. 289
"How Beautiful Thy Temples, Lord," *Hymns*, no. 288
"We Love Thy House, O God," *Hymns*, no. 247

SUMMARY

The First Presidency released a special letter to wards at the October 2018 general conference explaining that the elders quorum president and the Relief Society president of each ward are to assign a counselor whose responsibility will include temple and family history work. Ward members can assist and support efforts in the eternally important work of redeeming our dead.

President Russell M. Nelson challenged the sisters in the general Relief Society broadcast in October 2018 to establish a pattern of regular temple attendance and to prayerfully study temples in the scriptures and in the words of living prophets. He extended his challenge even further when he said, "Seek to know more, to understand more, to feel more about temples than you ever have before" ("Open the Heavens through Temple and Family History Work," *Ensign*, Nov. 2018). Surely this wise counsel also applies to the brethren in the Church.

Salvation is given to every living man and woman, but exaltation requires that everyone be baptized and receive temple ordinances. We can perform temple work for those who have lived on earth without hearing the gospel and receiving the saving ordinances. Our ancestors gave us the gift of life, and by doing their temple work we can help them gain eternal life. A merciful Father in Heaven allows us to receive those endowments for our kindred dead and make eternal blessings available to our ancestors who were not able to enter the temple for themselves.

As we research our family's history to identify our ancestors, the Lord will help us. He wants families to be together and has given us the tools we need and the sacred houses where they can be sealed. It is one of the most important works we can do here on earth. Our deceased loved ones are counting on us to help them with their eternal progression. If you want to have a spiritual experience, hasten your family history and temple work!

• •

QUOTES

➤ "Genealogies, family stories, historical accounts, and traditions . . . form a bridge between past and future and bind generations together in ways that no other keepsake can." (Dennis B. Neuenschwander, "Bridges and Eternal Keepsakes," *Liahona,* July 1999, 98–100.)

➤ "[The Lord] has trusted you by letting you hear the gospel in your lifetime, giving you the chance to accept the obligation to offer it to those of your ancestors who did not have your priceless opportunity. Think of the gratitude He has for those who pay the price in work and faith to find the names of their ancestors and who love them and Him enough to offer them eternal life in families, the greatest of all the gifts of God. He offered them an infinite sacrifice. He will love and appreciate those who paid whatever price they could to allow their ancestors to choose His offer of eternal life." (Henry B. Eyring, "Hearts Bound Together," *Ensign,* May 2005, 79.)

➤ "There exists a righteous unity between the temple and the home. Understanding the eternal nature of the temple will draw you to your family; understanding the eternal nature of the family will draw you to the temple." (Gary E. Stevenson, "Sacred Homes, Sacred Temples," *Ensign,* May 2009, 102.)

➤ "In the ordinances of the temple, the foundations of the eternal family are sealed in place." (Howard W. Hunter, "A Temple-Motivated People," *Liahona,* May 1995, 4.)

• •

GOSPEL ART

Adam and Eve Kneeling at an Altar, 4
Adam and Eve Teaching Their Children, 5
Jacob Blessing His Sons, 12
Boy Jesus in the Temple, 34
My Father's House, 52
Elijah Appearing in the Kirtland Temple, 95
Kirtland Temple, 117
Nauvoo Temple, 118
Salt Lake Temple, 119
Young Couple Going to the Temple, 120
Temple Baptismal Font, 121

• •

VIDEOS

"Time Well Spent": https://www.lds.org/media-library/video/2014-07-05
-time-well-spent

"Eternal Family—Paul": https://www.lds.org/media-library/video/2009-04
-062-eternal-family-paul

"Temples Bless the Living and the Dead": https://www.lds.org/media-library
/video/2010-07-108-temples-bless-the-living-and-the-dead

"RootsTech 2013 Family History Callings: First Hearts, Then Charts":
https://www.lds.org/media-library/video/2013-03-405-rootstech-2013
-family-history-callings-first-hearts-then-charts

"Why Mormons Do Family History": http://lds.org/media-library/video
/our-values

• •

OBJECT LESSONS

➤ Set out some bite-sized candy or fruit on a tray, and ask if there is anyone in the class who would like some. When a volunteer comes up to the front of the room, explain that he or she can have it but can't use any part of their body to pick it up. The volunteer may be clever and try various things, but the bottom line is that the treat cannot be picked up without the help of another volunteer. Talk about how this is similar to our kindred dead who want the saving ordinances but can't receive them without a physical body. We are the ones who can volunteer to help them receive their eternal treat!

- Invite your ward family history specialist to share some special experiences about binding heaven with earth as well as how the family history library works.
- Tell your class about open-air museums. They are all over Europe and give visitors a hands-on experience with how their ancestors lived in those countries centuries ago. You can find tons of video clips on YouTube by typing in the name of the country you want to learn about and then the words "open-air museum." The videos usually have music in the background as the camera scans the area. Some of them feature a host or tourist who tells you what is there to see and do. They're a lot of fun and bind your heart closer to your ancestors. When we do temple work for our kindred dead, we are creating a sacred seal that blesses individuals on both sides of the veil!

ARTICLES

Dallin H. Oaks, "Family History: In Wisdom and Order," *Ensign*, June 1989, 6–8.
David E. Sorensen, "The Doctrine of Temple Work," *Liahona*, Aug. 2002, 30.
Howard W. Hunter, "A Temple-Motivated People," *Liahona*, May 1995.
Stacy Vickery, "Temple Blessings Now and Eternally," *Liahona*, Sept. 2011.
Howard W. Hunter, "We Have A Work To Do," *Ensign*, Mar. 1995, 64–65.
Dennis B. Neuenschwander, *"Bridges and Eternal Keepsakes," Ensign*, May 1999, 83–85.

CHALLENGE

Watch the tutorial videos on the Church's "Family Tree" website at www.familysearch.org. Click on "Family Tree" in the top menu. If you don't have one already, create an account and begin researching the names of your ancestors to see where you can begin doing their temple work.

Think of creative ways to celebrate your family's history and honor your heritage. There are tons of ideas in my newest Kindle book *Ancestry: How to Research Your Family History and Climb Your Family Tree*. It is offered for free on Kindle Unlimited!

DOCTRINAL MASTERY PASSAGES

Old Testament

Genesis 1:26–27

Genesis 39:9

Exodus 20:3–17

Deuteronomy 7:3–4

2 Timothy 3:1–5

Job 19:25–26

New Testament

1 Corinthians 15:20–22

1 Corinthians 15:29

Doctrine and Covenants

D&C 131:1–4

D&C 137:7–10

2 Nephi 2:25

Moses 1:39

• •

PREACH MY GOSPEL

Pages 31–32, 47–50, 52–54, 85–86, 159–165

• •

NOTES

ℒesson 23

HEARING THE HOLY GHOST

. . . .

MUSIC

"The Holy Ghost," *Children's Songbook*, 105
"The Still Small Voice," *Children's Songbook*, 106
"Dearest Children, God Is Near You," *Hymns*, no. 96
"God of Power, God of Right," *Hymns*, no. 20
"Great Is the Lord," *Hymns*, no. 77
"The Spirit of God," *Hymns*, no. 2

. . . .

SUMMARY

It was a pleasure to hear from Elder Gerrit W. Gong during the October 2018 general conference. He gave us ideas on how to build campfires of faith and hear the Spirit more in our lives. He shared his heart when he said, "My testimony is—for those who seek, allow, and live for it—the dawn of faith, sometimes gradually, will come or can return. The light will come when we desire and seek it, when we are patient and obedient to God's commandments, when we are open to God's grace, healing, and covenants" ("Our Campfire of Faith," *Ensign*, Nov. 2018).

The Holy Ghost has been sent to us by a loving Heavenly Father to provide comfort, guidance, and a witness for truth. The Holy Ghost is a member of the Godhead and has a distinct mission to testify of the Father and the Son to our minds and hearts. The Holy Ghost is a personage of spirit that speaks to our souls, and by His power we are able to understand and live the gospel of Jesus Christ.

Everyone in the world can feel the influence of the Holy Ghost at certain times; however, the *gift* of the Holy Ghost is the privilege to receive His constant companionship and guidance by the laying on of hands. The gift of the Holy Ghost is bestowed upon a repentant person whose sins have been washed away at baptism. To hear the quiet promptings of the Holy Ghost, we must be obedient, humble, and prayerful. This great gift from a loving Father can bless us with guidance, comfort, and testimony.

QUOTES

- "The simplicity of this ordinance may cause us to overlook its significance. These four words—'Receive the Holy Ghost'—are not a passive pronouncement; rather, they constitute a priesthood injunction—an authoritative admonition to act and not simply to be acted upon." (David A. Bednar, "Receive the Holy Ghost," *Ensign*, Nov. 2010.)
- "We need the help of the Holy Ghost if we are to make our way safely through what the Apostle Paul called the 'perilous times' in which we now live." (Gerald N. Lund, "Opening Our Hearts," *Ensign*, May 2008.)
- "When the Prophet Joseph Smith was asked 'wherein [the LDS Church] differed . . . from the other religions of the day,' he replied that it was in 'the gift of the Holy Ghost by the laying on of hands, . . . [and] that all other considerations were contained in the gift of the Holy Ghost.'" (James E. Faust, "The Light in their Eyes," *Ensign*, Nov. 2005.)
- "The Holy Ghost . . . is our comforter, our direction finder, our communicator, our interpreter, our witness, and our purifier—our infallible guide and sanctifier." (Dallin H. Oaks, "'Always Have His Spirit,'" *Ensign*, Nov. 1996, 59–61.)
- "Testimony brings to us a knowledge that the gospel is true, but conversion by the Spirit brings something more." (Loren C. Dunn, "Fire and the Holy Ghost," *Ensign*, June 1995, 22–26.)
- "If [we] would open [our] hearts to the refining influence of this unspeakable gift of the Holy Ghost, a glorious new spiritual dimension would come to light." (Joseph B. Wirthlin, "The Unspeakable Gift," *Liahona*, May 2003, 26–29; or *Ensign*, May 2003, 26–29.)

GOSPEL ART

Boy Samuel Called by the Lord, 18
John the Baptist Baptizing Jesus, 35
The Liahona, 61

• •

VIDEOS

"Holy Host: Gift of Discernment": https://www.lds.org/media-library/video
/topics/holy-ghost
"The Unspeakable Gift of the Holy Ghost": http://www.lds.org/media-library
/video/2012-01-0010-the-unspeakable-gift-of-the-holy-ghost
"Feeling the Holy Ghost": http://www.lds.org/media-library/video/2012-01
-001-feeling-the-holy-ghost
"Having the Holy Ghost": http://www.lds.org/media-library/video/2012-01
-005-having-the-holy-ghost
There is an excellent three-part series called "Patterns of Light" by Elder
Bednar at http://www.lds.org/media-library/video/2012-01-011-patterns
-of-light-discerning-light.

• •

OBJECT LESSONS

⟿ Ask a volunteer to crush an empty soda can with only one hand. Most
people can do it. Next, ask the volunteer to crush a full soda can with one
hand. It won't work because the can is filled. Compare that to when we
are filled with the Holy Ghost—Satan can't crush us!

⟿ Show the class a variety of objects that involve air in some way: balloons,
a bicycle tire, a hair dryer, inflatable balls, an air pump, an aerosol can,
a fan, soap bubbles, etc. Ask the class what the objects have in common.
Explain that while we can't see air, we know it's there because of the
affects it has. We can't see the Holy Ghost because He doesn't have a
physical body, but we can feel His power and influence.

⟿ Demonstrate the difference between the Holy Ghost and the *gift* of the
Holy Ghost by using a flashlight. Everyone in the world can feel flashes
of inspiration from the Holy Ghost at times when they are receiving comfort, guidance, or a witness of truth; however, it often quickly fades away.
Turn the flashlight on and off. After you are baptized and given the *gift*
of the Holy Ghost, you have the privilege of having the Holy Ghost as a
constant companion. Turn on the flashlight, and keep it on. We can keep

our spiritual "batteries" charged and receive continuous light from the Holy Ghost if we live worthily.

* *

ARTICLES

Douglas L. Callister, "Seeking the Spirit of God," *Ensign*, Nov. 2000.

Neal A. Maxwell, "The Holy Ghost: Glorifying Christ," *Ensign*, July 2002.

James E. Faust, "Communion with the Holy Spirit," *Ensign*, Mar. 2002.

Loren C. Dunn, "Fire and the Holy Ghost," *Ensign*, June 1995.

Boyd K. Packer, "The Gift of the Holy Ghost: What Every Member Should Know," *Ensign*, Aug. 2006.

David A. Bednar, "That We May Always Have His Spirit to Be with Us," *Ensign*, May 2006.

James E. Faust, "The Gift of the Holy Ghost—A Sure Compass," *Ensign*, Apr. 1996.

* *

CHALLENGE

Doctrine and Covenants 8:2 gives us a pattern the Lord uses to help us recognize the Holy Ghost: "Yea, behold, I will tell you in your mind and in your heart, by the Holy Ghost, which shall come upon you and which shall dwell in your heart." Begin a "spiritual journal," in which you record special experiences when you felt the Holy Ghost in your life. Like Nephi's small plates, fill this new journal with experiences that built your faith and times when you saw the Lord's hand in your life. This special record will be a powerful heirloom and blessing and to you and to generations to come. If you notice large gaps of time between entries, you will be reminded to refocus your attention on spiritual matters.

* *

DOCTRINAL MASTERY PASSAGES

Book of Mormon
2 Nephi 32:3
Moroni 10:4–5

New Testament
James 1:5–6

Doctrine and Covenants
D&C 8:2–3
D&C 130:22–23

PREACH MY GOSPEL

Pages 18, 90–91

NOTES

Lesson 24

CHOOSING TO REMOVE NEGATIVE INFLUENCES

. . . .

MUSIC

"Choose the Right," *Hymns*, no. 239
"Choose the Right Way," *Children's Songbook*, 160
"Know This, That Every Soul Is Free," *Hymns*, no. 240
"I Will Follow God's Plan," *Children's Songbook*, 164
"Dare to Do Right," *Children's Songbook*, 158

. . . .

SUMMARY

In the October 2018 general conference, President Dallin H. Oaks discussed the importance of making wise choices as we organize our time and seek for truth in this life. He stated, "When we seek the truth about religion, we should use spiritual methods appropriate for that search: prayer, the witness of the Holy Ghost, and study of the scriptures and the words of modern prophets" ("Truth and the Plan," *Ensign*, Nov. 2018).

We live in the "Information Age," when our choices are innumerable. The right to choose between good and evil and to act for ourselves is called *agency*. It is a principle that existed before we came to earth and will continue to exist after we leave it. By following Jesus Christ, we are choosing eternal life and liberty. If we follow Satan, we are selecting evil and eternal captivity. The thirteenth article of faith encourages us to fill our lives with things that are 'lovely, virtuous, praiseworthy, and of good report. There is so much of that in the world today!

While we are free to make choices, we are not free to choose the consequences of our actions. What good is having someone who can walk on water if you don't follow in His footsteps?

• •

QUOTES

↪ "In this life we have to make many choices. Some are very important choices. Some are not. Many of our choices are between good and evil. The choices we make, however, determine to a large extent our happiness or our unhappiness, because we have to live with the consequences of our choices." (James E. Faust, "Choices," *Ensign*, May 2004.)

↪ "You were chosen to participate in His work at this time because He trusts you to make the right choices." (Randall L. Ridd, "The Choice Generation," *Ensign*, May 2014.)

↪ "Modern revelation makes it clear that agency is a gift from our Heavenly Father to allow us to choose obedience, which leads us to eternal life." (L. Lionel Kendrick, "Our Moral Agency," *Ensign*, Mar. 1996, 28–32.)

↪ "While the freedom to choose involves the risk of mistakes, it also offers the opportunity, through our Father's plan, to overcome them." (Spencer J. Condie, "Agency: The Gift of Choices," *Ensign*, Sept. 1995, 16–22.)

↪ "We are given the knowledge, the help, the enticement, and the freedom to choose the path of eternal safety and salvation. The choice to do so is ours." (Howard W. Hunter, "The Golden Thread of Choice," *Ensign*, Nov. 1989, 17–18.)

↪ "Ever and always [the Atonement] offers amnesty from transgression and from death if we will but repent. . . . Repentance is the key with which we can unlock the prison from inside . . . and agency is ours to use it." (Boyd K. Packer, "Atonement, Agency, Accountability," *Ensign*, May 1988, 69–72.)

• •

GOSPEL ART

The Lord Created All Things, 2
Building the Ark, 7
Ruth Gleaning in the Fields, 17
Calling of the Fishermen, 37
The Sermon on the Mount, 39
The Good Samaritan, 44
Mary and Martha, 45

• •

VIDEOS

There are many videos on the Church's website that address addiction and pornography and the steps to change and remove those harmful influences. You can find them all listed on one page at https://www.lds.org/media-library/video/categories/addiction.

"Help Others Move toward the Savior": https://www.lds.org/media-library/video/2017-01-002-help-others-move-toward-the-savior

"What's the Best Thing Parents Can Do to Protect Children from Negative Sexual Influences?": https://www.lds.org/media-library/video/2012-12-018-whats-the-best-thing-parents-can-do-to-protect-children-from-negative-sexual-influences

"Choices": https://www.lds.org/general-conference/2016/04/choices

"The Three Rs of Choice": https://www.lds.org/general-conference/2010/10/the-three-rs-of-choice

"Act for Themselves": https://www.lds.org/media-library/video/2012-08-1260-act-for-themselves

• •

OBJECT LESSONS

➤ Invite the class to close their eyes and listen to various kinds of music. Play short snippets of songs from multiple genres, like classical, country, jazz, hard rock, and pop, and music by the Tabernacle Choir at Temple Square. Ask the class members how each kind of music made them feel and why.

➤ Hold up pictures of various things (websites, movies, books, clothes, music, food, apps, etc.), and ask the class to apply the counsel in the thirteenth article of faith ("If there is anything virtuous, lovely, or of good report or praiseworthy, we seek after these things."). Give everyone a piece of paper that has "Yes" written on one side and "No" written on the other side. When you hold up the pictures of various items, ask them to hold up their signs to determine if it meets the definition of what it is we should be seeking in our lives.

➤ Give a volunteer a bag labeled "Good Choices" (filled with Legos). Give another volunteer a bag labeled "Bad Choices" (filled with broken sticks). Ask them to build the best house they can with what they were given. Talk about how it's difficult to build a good life from bad choices.

• •

ARTICLES

Glen C. Griffin and Victor B. Cline, "Screening Out the Garbage," *Ensign*, Aug. 1976.

Hadley Griggs, "Fireproofing Yourself against Negativity," *New Era*, Feb. 2017.

Aysia Tan, "No Neutral Ground: How Media Influences Us," *Ensign*, Sept. 2016.

Ronald W. Walker and D. Michael Quinn, "'Virtuous, Lovely, or of Good Report,'" *Ensign*, July 1977.

H. David Burton, "Let Virtue Garnish Your Thoughts," *Ensign*, Nov. 2009.

Richard G. Scott, "Removing Barriers to Happiness," *Ensign*, May 1998.

Howard W. Hunter, "The Golden Thread of Choice," *Ensign*, Nov. 1989.

Boyd K. Packer, "Atonement, Agency, Accountability," *Ensign*, May 1988.

• •

CHALLENGE

Our lives are ridiculously full and busy. Each day we choose what is most important to us by the things we fill our life with, whether intentionally or not. Make a list of all of the tasks you need to complete every day. Do those things bring you closer to or further from God? What things can you let go of? What new items could you add to show you choose righteousness over wickedness?

• •

DOCTRINAL MASTERY PASSAGES

Book of Mormon
1 Nephi 3:7
2 Nephi 2:27
2 Nephi 28:7–9
Jacob 2:18–19
Mosiah 3:19
Mosiah 4:30
Alma 34:32–34
Alma 41:10
Helaman 5:12
Moroni 7:16–17
Moroni 7:45

Old Testament
Exodus 20:3–17

Joshua 1:8
Isaiah 1:18

New Testament
Matthew 6:24
John 7:17
John 14:15
1 Corinthians 10:13
Revelation 20:12–13

Doctrine and Covenants
D&C 1:37–38
D&C 14:7
D&C 58:26–27

• •

PREACH MY GOSPEL

Pages 47–49, 66, 72, 75, 88, 150–151

• •

NOTES

_____

_____

_____

_____

_____

_____

Lesson 25

USING TECHNOLOGY
TO DO MORE GOOD

MUSIC

"Because I Have Been Given Much," *Hymns*, no. 219
"Love One Another," *Hymns*, no. 308
"Love One Another," *Children's Songbook*, 136
"'Tis Sweet to Sing the Matchless Love," *Hymns*, no. 177
"Truth Reflects upon Our Senses," *Hymns*, no. 273
"We Have Partaken of Thy Love," *Hymns*, no. 155

SUMMARY

When we spend more time on social media or other technology, we often become distracted and can't hear spiritual promptings. Elder Jeffrey R. Holland pointed out that the original Latin meaning of the word *amusement* is "a diversion of the mind intended to deceive" ("Sanctify Yourselves," *Ensign*, Nov. 2000). Satan uses entertainment and other media to distract us from what is truly important in life. We need to be careful how we choose to spend our time with technology. It can be the source of great good or spiritually damaging evil.

Sister Michelle D. Craig, first counselor in the Young Women General Presidency, spoke to the girls and women during the October 2018 general conference and reminded us, "Whether they are direct promptings or just impulses to help, a good deed is never wasted, for 'charity never faileth'—and is never the wrong response" ("Divine Discontent," *Ensign*, Nov. 2018).

Visit the Church's website to learn more about the #ShareGoodness campaign: https://www.lds.org/church/share/goodness. You'll find tips on how to start a conversation, where to find shareable Church content, and ideas on how to spread messages of goodness and truth.

• •

QUOTES

⚬ "This is your world, the world of the future, with inventions undreamed of that will come in your lifetime as they have in mine. How will you use these marvelous inventions? More to the point, how will you use them to further the work of the Lord?" (M. Russell Ballard, "Using New Media to Support the Work of the Church," BYU–Hawaii graduation ceremony, Dec. 2007.)

⚬ "Our responsibility is not to avoid media altogether or to merely reject negative media but to choose wholesome and uplifting media." (Aysia Tan, "No Neutral Ground: How Media Influences Us," *Ensign*, Sept. 2016.)

⚬ "As in life, the Internet will give you more and more of what you seek. If your desires are pure, the Internet can magnify them, making it ever easier to engage in worthy pursuits. But the opposite is also true." (Randall L. Ridd, "The Choice Generation," *Ensign*, May 2014.)

⚬ "Make sure that the choices you make in the use of new media are choices that expand your mind, increase your opportunities, and feed your soul." (M. Russell Ballard, "Sharing the Gospel Using the Internet," *Ensign*, July 2008.)

⚬ "Faced with an excess of information in the marvelous resources we have been given, we must begin with focus or we are likely to become like those in the well-known prophecy about people in the last days—"ever learning, and never able to come to the knowledge of the truth." (2 Tim. 3:7). We also need quiet time and prayerful pondering as we seek to develop information into knowledge and mature knowledge into wisdom." (Dallin H. Oaks, "Focus and Priorities," *Ensign*, May 2001, 83.)

⚬ "We do not know what marvels God will inspire people to create to help in His work of gathering His family. But whatever marvelous inventions may come, their use will require the Spirit working in people like you and me. This should not surprise us. After all, these are beloved sons and daughters of God. He will send whatever inspiration is needed to give them the opportunity to return to Him." (Henry B. Eyring, "Gathering the Family of God," *Ensign*, May 2017.)

• •

GOSPEL ART

• •

VIDEOS

"Taming Technology in the Home": https://www.lds.org/media-library/video/2017-06-0011-taming-technology-in-the-home

"Role of New Materials and Technologies in Personal Gospel Study": https://www.lds.org/media-library/video/2012-01-5070-role-of-new-materials-and-technologies-in-personal-gospel-study

"Social Media Guidelines": https://www.lds.org/media-library/video/2014-08-1040-social-media-guidelines

"What Parents Need to Know about Their Kids and Social Media": https://www.mormonchannel.org/watch/series/gospel-solutions-for-families/what-parents-need-to-know-about-their-kids-and-social-media

• •

OBJECT LESSONS

✏ Challenge the class to a listening game. Tell them to write down every fifth sentence they hear during one of the general conference talks. At the same time, play a popular song on the radio while you pretend to talk on your cell phone. Talk about how we are constantly being flooded with information and the attention of many different sources. Share ideas about how we can focus our minds and our time on those things that actually edify and enrich our lives.

✏ Invite someone in the class who has a blog or website to share how he or she is using technology to spread the gospel of Jesus Christ.

✏ Invite your class to follow the First Presidency and Twelve Apostles on their social media sites! Here is a list: https://www.lds.org/prophets-and-apostles/unto-all-the-world/social-media-and-the-brethren?lang=eng.

✏ Show the class how to download the Church's LDS Media Library app, and demonstrate how to find videos, music, and images, as well as how to organize media for offline teaching.

ARTICLES

"Sharing via Social Media": https://www.lds.org/church/share/sharing-the-gospel-via-social-media

"Families Should Discuss How to Use Social Media in Righteous Ways": https://www.lds.org/church/news/families-should-discuss-how-to-use-social-media-in-righteous-ways

"Apostle Offers Counsel about Social Media": https://www.lds.org/ensign/2015/01/news-of-the-church/apostle-offers-counsel-about-social-media

"How to Network through Social Media": https://www.ldsjobs.org/ers/ct/network-through-social-media

"How to Have a More Uplifting Experience on Social Media": https://www.mormon.org/blog/how-to-have-a-more-uplifting-experience-on-social-media

CHALLENGE

Apple recently released a time-tracking feature for iPhones that lets you to see how much time you spend on each app and set time restrictions. Choose to follow uplifting accounts, such as the official Church accounts, the Apostles' Twitter feeds, blogs written by faithful members of the Church, etc.

. . . .

DOCTRINAL MASTERY PASSAGES

Book of Mormon
1 Nephi 3:7
Jacob 2:18–19
Mosiah 2:17
Mosiah 4:30
Moroni 7:45

Old Testament
Leviticus 19:18

New Testament
Matthew 5:14–16
Matthew 25:40

Doctrine and Covenants
D&C 84:33–39
D&C 137:7–10

. . . .

PREACH MY GOSPEL

Pages 2, 8, 62, 87, 115, 118, 123–126, 168–169

. . . .

NOTES

_____

_____

_____

_____

_____

_____

_____

_____

_____

_____

_____

Website Resources

No need to reinvent the wheel, especially when you're using that wheel to drive on the information super highway! The internet is an endless resource of ideas, recipes, downloads, crafts, lesson material, music, and instructions for almost anything you'd like to do in your Relief Society or elders quorum Sunday lessons.

Allow me to give you a serious word of caution about doing online searches. If you enter "women" into a search engine, you will get suggestions for links to all kinds of horrible pornographic websites. You must type in "LDS women" or "Relief Society," and even then, look at the description of the site before you click on it!

• •

LDS WEBSITE RESOURCES

www.lds.org—The official website of The Church of Jesus Christ of Latter-day
    Saints. This should be your first stop on the web.
www.jennysmith.net
www.theideadoor.com
www.mormons.org
www.angelfire.com
www.mormonfind.com
www.lightplanet.com/mormons
www.ldsworld.com
www.ldsteach.com
www.JeanniGould.com
www.mormontown.org
www.sugardoodle.net
www.ldssplash.com
www.ldstoday.com

• •

MERCHANDISE

www.ldscatalog.com—Church distribution center to order materials
www.byubookstore.com
www.ldsliving.com
www.deseretbook.com
www.ctr-ring.com

. . . .

LDS RELIEF SOCIETY BLOGS

http://enrichmentideas.blogspot.com
http://thereliefsocietyblog.blogspot.com
www.hollyscorner.com/blog/lds-resources/relief-society
www.mormonmomma.com/index.php/category/church/relief-society
http://lds.families.com/blog/category/1071
http://segullah.org/daily-special/putting-the-relief-in-relief-society
http://feastupontheword blog.org/2009/07/27/coming-up-in-relief-society
    -and-melchizedek-priesthood-for-2010-and-2011
http://happyjellybeans.blogspot.com

. . . .

LDS BLOGS FOR MEN

https://mormoneldersquorum.blogspot.com
https://sacoeldersquorum.blogspot.com
https://leadingsaints.org/category/elders-quorum
www.MiddleagedMormonMan.com
https://rejoiceandbeexceedingglad.blogspot.com
www.GregTrimble.com
https://bycommonconsent.com

. . . .

INTERNET GROUPS

I highly recommend that you join a Yahoo Group. It's free to join, and you'll meet some of the nicest people around! People share helpful ideas and tips in a real-time setting. You can receive the e-mails individually or as a daily digest. Some groups are more active than others, so the quantity of e-mails will vary. No reason to reinvent the wheel when another great Relief Society or elders quorum teacher has already done it out there somewhere!

http://groups.yahoo.com/group/ReliefSociety-L
http://uk.groups.yahoo.com/group/Relief_SocietyLDS
http://groups.yahoo.com/group/ldsreliefsocietypresidency
http://groups.yahoo.com/group/LDSReliefSocietyMeetings
http://groups.yahoo.com/group/LDS_husbands
http://groups.yahoo.com/lds-tech-lessons
http://groups.yahoo.com/LDSDads
http://groups.yahoo.com/Mormon

CLIP ART

I'm thankful for talented artists who share their wonderful creations with me, since I have trouble drawing decent stick people! Here are some of those generous artists.

Most of the websites mentioned above, plus the following:

- www.christysclipart.com
- www.graphicgarden.com
- designca.com/lds
- www.coloringbookfun.com
- www.stums.org/closet/html/index.html
- www.oneil.com.au/lds/pictures.html
- lds.about.com/library/gallery/clipart/blclipart_gallery_subindex.htm
- www.free-clip-art.net
- www.coloring.ws/coloring.html
- www.apples4theteacher.com

MUSIC

www.lds.org/music
www.mormonchannel.org
https://www.lds.org/youth/music
www.ldsmusicians.com
www.yldsr.com
www.defordmusic.com
www.Radio.ldsmusicnow.com

http://lds.about.com/library/clipart/blnewera_music_1975.htm—Great index of all sheet music offered in the *New Era* and *Ensign* magazines from 1975 to 1989

www.ldsmusicworld.com

www.ldsmusictoday.com

www.ldsmusicsource.com

www.ldspianosolo.com

www.deseretbook.com/LDS-Music/Sheet-Music-Downloads/s/1395

About the Author

Trina Boice grew up in California and currently lives in Las Vegas, where she teaches online for Brigham Young University–Idaho in their amazing Pathway program.

In 2004 she was honored as the California Young Mother of the Year, an award that completely amuses her four sons. She earned two bachelor's degrees from BYU, where she competed on the speech and debate team and the ballroom dance team. She was president of the National Honor Society Phi Eta Sigma and served as ASBYU secretary of student community services.

Trina is currently a doctoral student at CTU and also studied at the University of Salamanca in Spain, later returning there to serve an LDS mission in Madrid for one and a half years.

She is a movie critic at www.MovieReviewMom.com and loves to travel, so she created www.EmptyNestTravelHacker.com, where she shares her travel hacks and tips. Check out her YouTube channels with both of those same names too!

She has a real estate license, travel agent license, two master's degrees, and a black belt in taekwondo, although she's the first one to admit she'd pass out from fright if she were ever really attacked by a bad guy.

She worked as a legislative assistant for a congressman in Washington, DC, and was given the "Points of Light" award and Presidential Volunteer Service Award for her domestic and international community service. She wrote a column called "The Boice Box" for a newspaper in Georgia, where she lived for fifteen years. She taught Spanish at a private high school and ran an appraisal business with her husband for twenty years. She currently writes for several newspapers and websites.

Trina was selected by KPBS in San Diego to be a political correspondent during the last presidential election. If she told you what she really did, she'd have to kill you.

A popular and entertaining speaker, Trina is the author of twenty-three books with another one hitting stores soon! You can read more about her books and upcoming events at www.trinasbooks.com.

Scan to visit

www.TrinasBooks.com